Pro-Life/
Pro-Peace

PRO-LIFE/ PRO-PEACE

Life-Affirming Alternatives to
Abortion, War, Mercy Killing, and
the Death Penalty

Lowell O. Erdahl

AUGSBURG Publishing House • Minneapolis

PRO-LIFE/PRO-PEACE
Life-Affirming Alternatives to Abortion, War, Mercy Killing, and the Death Penalty

Scripture quotations unless otherwise noted are from the Revised Standard Version of the Bible, copyright 1946, 1952, and 1971 by the Division of Christian Education of the National Council of Churches.

Scripture quotations marked NEB are from the New English Bible. Copyright The Delegates of the Oxford University Press and The Syndics of the Cambridge University Press, 1961, 1970. Reprinted by permission.

Scripture quotations marked NIV are from the Holy Bible, New International Version. Copyright 1978 by the New York International Bible Society. Used by permission of Zondervan Bible Publishers.

Scripture quotations marked NAB are from the New American Bible, copyright Confraternity of Christian Doctrine, Washington, D.C.

Library of Congress Cataloging-in-Publication Data

Erdahl, Lowell O.
   PRO-LIFE/PRO-PEACE.
   Bibliography: p.

   1. Social ethics.   2. Pro-life movement.   3. Pacifism.
4. Peace. I. Title.
HM216.E67   1986   179'.7   86-3552
ISBN 0-8066-2209-1

Manufactured in the U.S.A.   APH 10-5240

  2   3   4   5   6   7   8   9   0   1   2   3   4   5   6   7   8   9   0

Other books by Lowell Erdahl:

Ten for Our Time: A New Look at the Ten Commandments

Be Good to Each Other: An Open Letter on Marriage
  (coauthored with Carol Erdahl)

*To pro-life and pro-peace friends
who are often at odds with each other
and to pacifist friends
whose witness challenges us all*

CONTENTS

PREFACE

Many of my pro-life friends don't like my views on war and capital punishment, and many pro-peace friends don't like my stands on abortion and mercy killing. These differences reflect the sharp division that exists within the Christian community and society at large, between those working for the abolition of war and capital punishment and those equally committed to oppose abortion and euthanasia. This conflict undermines the effectiveness of both efforts and decreases the likelihood that either will be successful.

This book is an open letter to my friends on both sides of this great divide. I hope that it will help them to understand my position and to be more understanding of one another.

From a wider perspective, what I have written is intended for all who are wrestling with these vital issues of life and death. I hope that it will help persons of all persuasions, and especially Christians, to stand united in opposition to unjustifiable abortion, war, mercy killing, and executions, and in affirmation of responsible alternatives to the institutions of death.

My purpose is to be persuasive, but I am content to be provocative. This is not an academic dissertation claiming all answers to these complex matters. It has been written—almost literally—on the run, and represents one pilgrim's present concerns and convictions. I have much to learn, and welcome readers' responses to increase my understanding.

I hope I am wrong in some of my convictions. I fear, for example, that continuing the arms race is likely to devastate humanity. Like a person fearful of having cancer, I would be delighted to know that my fears are unfounded. I would like to believe that God wills every new bomb and missile and that they are creating a world of lasting justice, peace, and freedom, but I cannot do so. I am, therefore, compelled to oppose the institutions of death and to affirm alternative ways of life.

I may also be wrong in the conviction that there are tragic, exceptional circumstances in which the taking of life is justifiable. Absolute pacifists, who reject all taking of life, may be correct. On the basis of the New Testament, it is easier to prove that Jesus was a pacifist than that he was a comfortable adherent of any of our denominations, but I am not yet persuaded that the will of God requires renunciation of killing in all circumstances.

I am grateful for Christian and humanitarian pacifism and am mindful that the word *pacifist* expresses commitment to act for peace and not to being passive. The pacifist witness confronts and convicts but has not yet fully convinced me. When one peace advocate declared that "I can only work with pure pacifists," I had to confess that "I'm not purely anything." Since I oppose the institutions of death while acknowledging tragic situations in which it may be justifiable to take human life, I see myself in the mainstream of the just/unjust-taking-of-life tradition.

Through application of the basic principles of this tradition, I have come to many of the convictions of those who call themselves pacifists and pro-lifers. Having felt at home, but not always comfortable, within both peacemaking and pro-life communities, I have come to believe that there is common ground on which these groups can come together. We need not agree on everything, but we must overcome the division that keeps us from being united in work and witness for life in fullness for all God's children—the born and the unborn, those living today and all who will live after us.

I am grateful for pro-life and pro-peace people who have expressed the unity we have with one another. I think especially of leaders of the Roman Catholic church such as Joseph Cardinal Bernardin, who has affirmed "The Seamless Garment" of life concerns; the editors of *Sojourner's* magazine; members of groups like Prolifers for Survival; individuals such as Senator Mark Hatfield, Steve Levicoff (author of *Building Bridges: The Prolife Movement and the Peace Movement*), George Muedeking (former editor of *The Lutheran Standard*), Colman McCarthy of the *Washington Post* and Nat Hentoff of *The Village Voice,* who have sought to be consistently life-affirming and death denying. I pray that pro-life and pro-peace people will increasingly stand together in such united witness for life.

Suggestions for specific action are included in the closing chapter. Two appendices—"Questions and Suggestions for Reflection and Discussion" and "Resources and References for Further Study and Mutual Support"—are also provided. I hope that these will be helpful to congregational study groups and that continued consideration of the themes discussed in this book will provoke conversation, commitment, and concerned action for the life of persons and the life of the world.

I am grateful to Myrwood Bagne, Joan and Tom Duke, Ed Fehskins, Jean Hawkinson, Jan Krocheski, Pat Markie, Maggie Pharris, Myron Schrag, Paul Sponheim, Jeff Rohr, Muriel Vaughan, Ted Vinger, and Tom Witt for their diverse and often opposing reactions to what I have written; to Kathy Malchow for her skill in preparing the manuscript; and to my wife Carol, for her support and patience while this project robbed precious hours from our too limited time together.

1 THE PRO-LIFE PRINCIPLE

Life has value. The higher the form of life the higher its value. We swat flies without remorse but do not lightly kill our pet cats and dogs. Something deep within us resonates to Albert Schweitzer's experience of "reverence for life"—above all, reverence for human life.

We sometimes say of others that "for them life is cheap" and in so doing consign them to a status less than fully human. We sense that to devalue life is to degrade and even dehumanize ourselves.

Reverence for life is the perspective of no single race or religion. It is as universal as the love of parents for their children. Its absence, like the absence of parental love, is recognized to be a pathological condition. Only psychopaths and sociopaths can without remorse destroy the lives of others.

God affirms life

While Christianity has no monopoly on reverence for life, it is a central Christian affirmation. In Jesus we see that God is on the side of life. Jesus came that we "may have life, and may have it in all its fullness" (John 10:10 NEB). Through the witness of the New Testament we see Jesus living out that reason for being. Jesus was consistently life affirming—always seeking to enable and ennoble the lives of others. Jesus not only fed the hungry, healed the sick, and gave hope to the hopeless; he also opposed those intent on taking life. Jesus stopped the execution of an adulterous woman (John 8:10) and told an impulsive defender to put away his sword (Matt. 26:52).

Jesus not only affirms the Old Testament law: "You shall love your neighbor as yourself" (Lev. 19:18 and Matt. 22:39); he also declares "A new commandment I give to you, that you love one another; even as I have loved you" (John 13:34). In giving the Golden Rule, "Always treat others as you would like them to treat you," Jesus declares "that is the Law and the prophets" (Matt. 7:12 NEB). In his command to "love one another as I have loved you" Jesus goes beyond "the Law and the prophets." In the old commandment the standard is the love of self; in the new commandment the standard is the love of Christ. By the old standard the masochist who desires punishment would be justified in inflicting punishment on others. No such interpretation is possible with Jesus' new commandment. When wrestling with the specific issues of life and death, we rightly seek guidance from the Golden Rule and can appropriately ask, "If I were in that person's situation would I want someone to kill me?" But in light of Jesus' new commandment we must also ask, "In taking this life, will I be loving another as Christ loves me?"

Old Testament perspectives

Since Jesus' new commandment at least limits, if not prohibits, all violence and killing, many Christians seek support for the taking of life primarily from the Old Testament. But even if we had no Scripture but the Old Testament, there would be no justification for idolatrous dependence on military power. Victory in the wars of the Old Testament was never correctly understood to be a human achievement. The conquest was God's doing: "I gave them into your hand . . . . it was not by your sword or by your bow" (Josh. 24:11-12). When Gideon assembled 32,000 men to battle the Midianites, the Lord said to Gideon, "The people with you are too many for me to give the Midianites into their hand, lest Israel vaunt themselves against me, saying, 'My own hand has delivered me' " (Judg. 7:2), and all but 300 were sent home. When David confronted Goliath, he declared, "The Lord saves not with sword and spear; for the battle is the Lord's and he will give you into our hand" (1 Sam. 17:47).

The Old Testament condemns excessive reliance on military power and reveals it to be idolatry. Jesus, however, goes even further and specifically rejects obedience to vengeful Old Testament precepts and unloving practices: "You have heard that it was said, 'An eye for an eye and a tooth for a tooth.' But I say to you, Do not resist one who is evil. But if anyone strikes you on the right cheek, turn to him the other also . . . . You have heard that it was said, 'You shall love your neighbor and hate your enemy.' But I say to you, Love your enemies and pray for those who persecute you" (Matt. 5:38-39, 43-44). These words of Jesus remind us that some Old Testament and rabbinic precepts are sub-Christian as well as pre-Christian, and, in light of the timeless elements of Hebrew teaching, sub-Jewish as well.

Those committed to obey and emulate everything in the Old Testament had better not read Lev. 20:9, which declares, "Everyone who curses his father or mother shall be put to death," or Num. 15:31-37 which tells of Moses' conviction concerning a man whom he believed God commanded to be stoned to death for having gathered sticks on the Sabbath, or Num. 31:17-18, which declares that the victors in war were to "kill every male among the little ones, and kill every woman who has known man by lying with him. But all the young girls who have not known man by lying with him, keep alive for yourselves."

Christians who seek to justify the taking of life on the basis of the Old Testament would be horrified to learn of fellow Christians who were practicing concubinage or polygamy on the basis of similar Old Testament interpretation. Preachers who regularly evoke Old Testament examples in support of war and capital punishment would be expelled from the ministry if they were to teach and practice a similar understanding of the Old Testament regarding sexual behavior. Why will a Christian congregation applaud a pastor for using the Old Testament in support of killing but be appalled if the same arguments were used in favor of prostitution and polygamy? Is all Old Testament teaching and example concerning killing eternal, while all of its precepts and practices concerning sexual behavior only temporal? Or are sexual sins really more grievous than the taking of life?

In defense of killing, many correctly state that the commandment "You shall not kill" (Exod. 20:13 and Deut. 5:17) did not prohibit war and capital punishment and was understood to mean "You shall not commit murder," but what Christian congregation would permit a similar interpretation of "You shall not commit adultery" (Exod 20:14), which in its original meaning guaranteed a husband's property right to sole possession of each wife but did not prohibit his own sexual activity with other wives, concubines, and prostitutes? If we are going to insist upon a New Testament interpretation of the commandment regarding adultery, should we not require a similar interpretation of the commandment regarding killing? Is not Christ, who is Lord of all, also Lord of the Bible and our supreme guide in understanding God's Word for our lives?

Those who believe that the prohibition against killing applies to individuals but not governments should ponder this statement:

How many does it take to metamorphose wickedness into righteousness? One man must not kill. If he does it is murder. Two, ten, one hundred men acting on their own responsibility must not kill. If they do it is still murder. But a state or nation may kill as many as it pleases and it is no murder. It is just, necessary, commendable and right. Only get people enough to agree to it, and the butchery of myriads of human beings is perfectly innocent. But how many men does it take? That is the question. Just so with theft, robbery, burglary, and other crimes . . . A whole nation may commit them. . . . But how many does it take? Why may not one, ten, or one hundred men, violate God's law, when a great number may do so?[1]

"How many does it take?" is a simple but profoundly significant question. It casts doubt on the validity of much "two kingdom" thinking that gives governments the right to act in ways that are clearly sinful for individuals and smaller groups. How many does it take before a person can call himself a prince or a group can elect a president with authority to transform sin into righteousness? This question underscores the distinction between responsible personal morality and the officially institutionalized immorality that I believe to be at the heart of humanity's worst violations of the pro-life principle.

Stewards of life

Each of us is a steward of life—our personal life, the life of every loved one, and the corporate life of the human family. Dr. Helen Caldecott has suggested that we look to the stars and wonder, "Is there other life in this vast universe?" Perhaps there is, but maybe there isn't. Ours may be the only thinking, dreaming, praying, loving, hoping life in all of God's vast creation. We are stewards of that life, trustees of the most precious gift of God's creation.

Love creates life. We are created to so live with love that life in fullness may abound within us and through us to others. As stewards of life we are concerned with everything, including politics, that affects the lives of others. We are mindful that the issues of life and death are moral and theological and not just political. They relate to the wellsprings of our faith and morality. Human failure to live as a responsible steward of life may be a crime against humanity. Christian failure to fulfill that stewardship is also a sin against God and against the brothers and sisters whom we have been created and redeemed to love.

The pro-life principle calls us to reverence life, to support everything that enhances and ennobles life and to oppose everything that degrades and destroys life. That means standing in basic support of education, art, healing, beauty, and all else that gives life meaning, hope, and joy. It also means that we stand in basic opposition to everything that diminishes meaning and joy and that threatens at any stage of human existence to snuff out the flame of life. As human beings and as Christians we say *yes!* to life and all that is life giving and we say *no!* to death and all that is death dealing.

The fact that there are tragic, exceptional circumstances in which the taking of life may be justifiable does not cancel the pro-life principle. Those exceptions prove the rule. The tragedy occurs when the exceptions become the rule.

2 LIFE AGAINST LIFE

Having affirmed reverence for life, what do we do when one life threatens to harm or destroy another? It is one thing to declare general support for the pro-life principle; it is quite another to face the specific dilemmas of life against life. Now we can no longer simply affirm life in general. Now we must choose: This life or that life?

There is no escape from the anguish of such a decision. Our situations are sometimes similar to *Sophie's Choice* in William Styron's moving novel of that title. Sophie stands before a concentration camp officer with her two children. One child will live; the other will die. The choice is hers. If she will not choose, both children will die.

Such are the agonizing dilemmas that at times confront us. A baby growing in its mother's womb threatens to destroy her life. A vengeful maniac goes berserk and starts shooting everyone in sight. An advancing army threatens to enslave or to kill us. What then do we do?

In such situations most Christians, as least since the fourth century, have argued that it is justifiable to take life in order to save life. They have held that an abortion is justified to save the mother's life, that it is right to kill a person bent on murder, and that it may be justifiable to kill the soldiers of an invading army.

When confronted by such clear alternatives, most of us, like Sophie, are compelled to choose one life over another. In retrospect we may relive that moment a thousand times and wonder if we did the right thing, but we will usually grant that we were forced to choose. Our grief, as a soldier who had killed in warfare once confided to me, will not be ''over what I did but over the fact that I had to do it.'' For him there was then—and still, would be now—no alternative. He confessed that what he had done was terrible. It involved the choice of life over life, and now, years later, he was still in anguish, not over what he had done but over the necessity of having had to do it. At the same time, it was also clear that grief was mingled with guilt. He sensed that he was part of a community and that in some measure he shared in corporate irresponsibility for having failed to create an alternative to his terrible choice. That guilt witnesses to a wider dimension of our dilemma. Somewhere, somehow, there was a failure. Someone could have done something—perhaps there was even something he himself could have done—that would have spared him the agony of that terrible choice. Much of this book is a quest for those alternatives—not only in times of crisis, but also to prevent the crisis from occurring.

Dilemmas of life

If all of the dilemmas of life against life involved clearly focused choices, there would be much anguish but relatively little debate concerning the issues of life and death. When one life threatens the physical destruction of another, the situation, while agonizing, is comparatively clear. Almost instinctively, we place a value on each of those lives. The life of the mother is considered more precious than that of her unborn child. The would-be murderer is less valued than that of the intended victim. The lives of our citizens under seige are regarded to be of greater worth than those of the invading army.

Our choices, however, are not always so sharply focused. What do we do when one life threatens not to destroy, but to harm or distress another? The developing pregnancy, for example, may not endanger the mother's life, but it could hinder her ability to provide for the welfare of her family, or her social and economic well-being, or her desire to pursue a new vocation. The invading army may not threaten the lives of the country's inhabitants. Their freedom to govern themselves, rather than their physical existence, is at stake. The competing values are not life versus life, but liberty versus slavery, or at least the choice of one government versus another. If it is justifiable to kill a soldier bent on conquest or massacre, is it also justifiable to kill a person intent on liberation? We glory in the heroes of the American Revolution and never doubt that they were justified in killing the British, who were about as accommodating as any "oppressor" could be. Did the civility of the British then give the Redcoats justification for killing the American revolutionaries?

In responding to such questions, most will agree that the taking of life is sometimes, but certainly not always, justifiable. An abortion in the third month of pregnancy to save the life of the mother? Yes! A sixth-month abortion to avenge her husband's affair? No! Killing the murderer who is shooting to kill everyone in sight? Yes! Killing the shoplifter in a candy store? No! Killing the soldiers defending Auschwitz? Yes! Killing the liberators of Auschwitz? No!

Contextual considerations

Only those who take the absolute position that it is never right to take life in any circumstances are free from wrestling with the factors unique to the circumstances. Although many criticize "situational" or "contextual" ethics, few can conscientiously avoid consideration of the specific factors in every situation. There are no rules that apply in every context. Nor are there any simple answers to free us from the dilemmas of agonizing choice.

Therefore, we long for criteria and guidelines concerning factors that make the taking of life either justifiable or unjustifiable. In the history of the Christian church such criteria have been most specifically stated in relation to justifiable/unjustifiable participation in warfare and there have also been debates concerning similar criteria relative to justifiable versus unjustifiable abortion, mercy killing, and capital punishment.

Even without specific guidelines, all who are motivated by profound reverence for life will oppose the taking of life in any but extreme circumstances. Most of us will agree that there are tragic, exceptional situations in which the value to be preserved justifies the taking of life, but we will not grant that any person has an inherent right to take the life of another. While granting the tragic exceptions, consistently pro-life people will reject every established practice that takes life without requiring the intellectual and moral struggle demanded of such a decision. We will most emphatically oppose legally and/or culturally institutionalized killing to solve personal, societal, and international problems.

3 WHEN THE EXCEPTIONS BECOME THE RULE

To introduce and illustrate the main point of this chapter, I invite you to ask yourself: (1) Is it ever right to tell a lie? and (2) Is it ever right to steal?

Most of us will probably answer yes to both questions. We likely agree that it was right that lies were told to save Jews from extermination and that it would be right to steal the gun from a would-be murderer or to rob the rich if there were no other way to feed our starving children. Having granted the acceptability, and even the necessity, of lying and stealing in such exceptional circumstances does not, however, mean that we must also agree that it would be right for a society to legalize and affirm lying and stealing. There is a great difference between granting the necessity of falsehood or theft in specific, exceptional circumstances and supporting an established practice of lying and stealing. To accept the one does not necessitate approval of the other.

Slavery and cannibalism provide similar illustrations of the difference between the exceptional and the institutional. Note how the 13th amendment to the United States Constitution clearly rejects the continued establishment of slavery as an accepted institution while permitting one form of "involuntary servitude" in one kind of exceptional circumstance: "Neither slavery nor involuntary servitude, *except as a punishment for crime whereof the party shall have been duly convicted,* shall exist within the United States, or any place subject to their jurisdiction" (emphasis added). Believing in "slavery" for criminals does not necessitate support for the economic and political institution of slavery within society. Also recall those who survived a plane crash in the Andes by eating portions of the frozen bodies of those killed in the crash. I believe that such cannibalism was justified in that exceptional situation, but I certainly do not advocate the establishment of cannibalism as general practice. Affirming the *exceptional* does not necessitate support for the *institutional.*

What is permissible, or even required, in exceptional circumstances need not, and often should not, become accepted practice. The exceptions may prove the rule, but they should not become the rule. When this happens, that which should be rare becomes regular, an aberration becomes acceptable, the exceptional becomes established and institutionalized.

The institutions of death

The institution of slavery has, thankfully, been abolished, and neither lying, stealing, nor cannibalism have become accepted, established practice among us. But there have been similar shifts from the exceptional to the institutional in regard to the taking of life. Prior to the Supreme Court's *Roe* v. *Wade* decision in 1973, it was generally understood that abortions were to be performed only in circumstances of tragic necessity. The specific definitions of that necessity varied, but abortion itself was considered to be an exceptional practice. With *Roe* v. *Wade* the exceptional became institutional. That which was once permitted in tragic, exceptional circumstances has now become "the right" of any pregnant woman during at least the first two-thirds of her pregnancy. By refusing to protect the unborn prior to viability, our society has in effect institutionalized abortion on demand. The exceptional has become an approved and established practice.

A similar shift from the exceptional to the institutional in regard to Christian participation in war began about the time of St. Augustine. This is not to say that Augustine and others who developed the just/unjust-war theories were themselves responsible for it. They were clear that Christian participation in war was to be exceptional and was permissible only when specific criteria were met. In practice, however, those criteria were soon forgotten, and justifiable warfare became whatever battle one's own country was currently fighting.

The advocates of justifiable warfare had no intention of, in effect, licensing all Christians to be warriors. They stressed that such participation was an exception to be granted only to those who after careful study, prayer, and deliberation found just cause to do so. In practice, however, the just-war theory was turned on its head. Christians came to understand that they could, and even should, *always go to war* when called on to do so, *except in unusual circumstances*. Christian participation in war and war making became the rule rather than the exception.

The consequence has been centuries of Christian slaughter, not only of pagans, but often each other, in obedience to the commands of tribal and national leaders. Questions related to the justifiability of particular conflicts have seldom been raised by anyone, including the leaders of the Christian community. As a result, war making, which was universally shunned by nearly all Christians for the first 300 years after Jesus, has had the support of most Christians ever since.

During the Vietnam War, a religious leader stated that since he was unable to reject Christian participation in all wars, he believed it was inappropriate for him to oppose this particular conflict. But, as illustrated in relation to lying, stealing, slavery, and cannibalism, supporting specific actions in exceptional circumstances does not necessitate acceptance of their established practice. One need not be a pacifist to oppose Christian participation in an unjust war. Nor need one believe that abortion can never be justified in order to oppose the established practice of abortion on demand.

A tragic error

I believe that this shift from the exceptional to the institutional is Christianity's—and humanity's—most tragic error in regard to the issues of life and death. We have somehow come to believe that since we could not oppose the taking of life in any and all circumstances, we were thereby compelled to support, or at least condone, its establishment within society. Believing in the necessity of abortion in tragic circumstances, we have given our support, or silent acquiescence, to abortion in almost all circumstances. Believing in the possibility of a just war, we have gone on to bless almost all war making, until we are now witnessing the militarization of the planet and the development of ironic means of "defense" that threaten our survival not only as individuals and nations but as a species.

Believing it just and responsible for police officers to kill a dangerous criminal, some countries and many states within our country have legally established capital punishment in order to kill sick and sinful people who have already been removed from society. Believing it unnecessary to use all available heroic measures to prolong life in all circumstances of terminal illness, we seem to be moving toward abandonment of efforts to prolong life in many situations and even to deliberately terminating it in others. Here, too, in regard to both mercy killing and the death penalty, we need to beware lest that which is permissible or necessary in exceptional cases become the established and institutionalized practice.

The slippery slopes

One way to avoid the slide from the acceptance of killing on rare occasions to its becoming acceptable and commonplace is to refuse to step onto the slippery slope—that is, to take a legalistic position that denies the validity of any exceptions. Regarding abortion, for example, this is the position of those few who maintain that all abortions are wrong and should be illegal, including those performed to save the life of the mother. The absolute pacifists take a comparable stand in relation to Christian participation in warfare. They believe that a Christian should refuse to kill another human being even if there is no other means of stopping that person from killing others. When asked, "What would you do if someone came to kill your family?" some will reply, "We would kneel and pray."

Those of us who do not share this conviction need the witness of these committed and often courageous people. If humanity continues to make war until we exterminate the species, it will be evident that the world would have been better off if everyone had knelt and prayed rather than supporting any form of taking of life. Nevertheless, most of us, including those pacifists who affirm police power while denying military power, cannot commit ourselves to absolute rejection of killing in all circumstances. Therefore, we must continue to struggle on the slippery slopes of these complex issues, doing all we can to limit the occasions of exceptional killing, to dismantle the established institutions of death, and to create in their place institutions of life.

In the following chapters we will consider problems inherent in the established practices of abortion, war, mercy killing, and capital punishment. My chief concern, however, is not just to oppose these practices but to find better ways of coping with circumstances that prompt their consideration. I believe that there are moral and functional life-affirming alternatives to these institutions of death. In the following chapters we will seek to explore them together.

4 ABORTION AND ITS PRO-LIFE ALTERNATIVES

Few issues, except slavery and the Vietnam War, have so divided the American people as has abortion. Many pro-life people regard abortion, except to save the life of the mother, as a sin against God and a crime against humanity. Some compare abortion in the United States with Hitler's death camps, and the 1973 *Roe* v. *Wade* case with the Dred Scott decision of 1857, which declared slaves to be property without constitutional rights. Other pro-choice people regard a woman's "right" to have an abortion as inherent to her full humanity and beyond the legitimate challenge of church, state, or husband. Many feminists consider commitment to abortion rights to be the hallmark of women's liberation. A clear, pro-life or pro-choice stance has become a litmus test of political purity, and elections have been won and lost on the basis of this single issue.

This chapter is an attempt to be faithful to the pro-life principle while at the same time recognizing that there are tragic, exceptional circumstances in which abortion is justifiable.

It is essential to distinguish between the ethical and legal dimensions of this complex and agonizing question. Therefore, we will first consider matters of Christian morality and then ask if "there oughta be a law." Christian responsibility in relation to abortion requires new attitudes and convictions as well as new laws. In fact, it is doubtful that changing laws will immediately result in a dramatic decrease in the number of abortions. Whatever happens in court or Congress, we seem destined to live with a tangle of judicial appeals and legislative battles over abortion for the foreseeable future.

In quest of common ground

We begin by seeking common ground on which to stand together as we discuss and debate this issue. We share a common sorrow over the million and a half abortions performed annually in the United States. We confess shared abhorrence for abortions, not only because of what they do to the unborn, but also to the women who have them. Although we may differ concerning its value in relation to the needs of the mother, can't we agree that from the moment of conception, the unborn is a wonder of God's creation worthy of reverence appropriate to its Creator and its potential destiny? At the same time, we share compassionate reverence for every woman oppressed with an unwanted pregnancy. Indeed, is not this dual reverence at the very heart of the abortion dilemma? One life is perceived to threaten another; if that were not true, there would be no problem.

As we stand together as God's people in Christ, we seek to focus on solutions to the problem and not just on each other's faults. Whatever our present position, we pray for openness to the will of God and for the wisdom, compassion, and courage to see and do what is right. None of us has all the answers. We need to listen and learn as well as speak and teach. As we do so, we may discover ways in which we can work with and not just against each other.

Facts of life

Professor Howard Hong of St. Olaf College taught us never to argue about empirically verifiable facts, and I hope that we need not argue about the biological facts of prenatal development. One fact is that human life begins at conception, and another is that the union of egg and sperm does not immediately constitute a fully developed human being. There are some obvious, and many not so obvious, stages in development toward full humanity, which from a Christian perspective is not attained (or rather *obtained* by the grace of God) in fullness until resurrection life. The single cell formed at conception is different from any other in the mother's body and contains coded information received from both father and mother that will determine the color of eyes and skin and all the other qualities received through inheritance. As the fertilized egg travels slowly down the fallopian tube toward the uterus it divides into 2 cells, then 4, 8, 16, 32, 64, and so on. Sometimes, during this first phase of development a dramatic division occurs that will result in identical twins. About one week after fertilization the tiny sphere of cells will have reached the womb. It will have about another week to implant itself in the lining of the uterus. It is estimated that about one-fourth fail to do so and, without the mother's awareness of having conceived, end their brief existence through her regular menstrual cycle.

Following implantation, there is rapid differentiation of the embryo into separate organs, and by six weeks after fertilization all of the internal organs are present in a rudimentary stage of development. Cardiac activity begins in about the fourth week, and there is electrical activity in the brain by the sixth. By the eighth week the skeleton begins to form, and fingers and toes are recognizable. After this point no new major structures will be added. By 12 to 20 weeks muscle and nerve development will enable movement felt by the mother, which in earlier times was called "quickening."

By about 26 weeks, about 10% of all fetus are "viable"—that is, able to survive outside the uterus without extraordinary medical care. This percentage increases rapidly with each passing day as the pregnancy moves toward full term. Improvements in the care of the prematurely born have made postbirth survival possible several weeks earlier than was true only a few years ago. Artificial wombs and embryo transplants may reduce the age of viability to the early weeks of pregnancy. It has also very recently become possible to capture the first cells of life for implantation in the womb of a host mother.

The question of value

The abortion controversy swirls around the question, When does human life begin? If we will agree that the answer does not automatically resolve the abortion dilemma, can we not also agree on the basis of both the biological facts and the biblical witness that human life begins at conception? Human development is a continuum from the moment of fertilization, which for faith is an act of divine creation through the reproductive process.

Asserting this fact and affirming this faith does not, however, answer the question of the appropriate value and degree of reverence for life appropriate for the unborn at every stage of development. Although this question is hotly debated, honest conversation again reveals areas of agreement. We all agree, for example, that human life has value before as well as following birth, and many will also concur that the developing unborn is to be reverenced and protected more highly in the seventh month of development than on the seventh day. Few advocate abortions in the seventh month, but most believe it appropriate for a teenage rape victim to receive a medication to prevent implantation if conception has occurred.

It is also obvious that the value parents place on the unborn is determined not only by its state of development, but by their desire, or lack of desire, for a child. When good friends who have been trying for years to get pregnant are successful, we rejoice with them over a four-week pregnancy, and we grieve if we learn a week later that "Mary lost their baby." In a similar way, the new medical specialty of fetology, which treats the fetus as a patient worthy of medical care, must convince us all that the unborn is neither a glob of worthless or tumorous tissue, nor the property of the bearer over which she has the sole right of life and death. Every decision concerning abortion involves at least two realities worthy of value—the mother and her developing unborn.

If we agree that no one, including the mother, has an inherent right to end the life of the unborn, we will likely also concur that there is at least one circumstance in which it is justifiable to do so—namely, when the pregnancy threatens the life of the mother. Many will list other situations in which they believe that abortion is also justifiable, such as pregnancies resulting from rape or incest; those threatening the mental, emotional, family, and economic, as well as physical, health of the mother; and pregnancies giving evidence of significant deformity in the unborn. Noting these situations is not to suggest criteria for justifiable abortions, but to indicate that we are approaching the abortion question within the context of the pro-life principle, which affirms reverence for life while recognizing the exceptional circumstances in which the taking of life, in this case prebirth life, may be justifiable.

Exception or rule?

The real tragedy concerning abortion is not that there are tragic, exceptional circumstances in which women, after thought, prayer, and consultation, choose to have abortions, but that abortion has become an established and institutionalized practice. There will always be debate concerning the so-called hard cases, but these are not the basic problem. The real problem is that hundreds of thousands of abortions are being performed each year in the United States (and millions more around the world) without careful thought, prayer, and consultation, and often without full awareness of what so-called termination of pregnancy actually involves. We should also note that pro-choice people often use "hard-case" arguments that support abortion in exceptional circumstances, but which do not prove that it should become the rule.

In the centuries since war became an institutionalized and accepted practice, millions of Christians have marched off to battle without even asking if it were justifiable to do so. Within only a few years something similar has happened in regard to abortion. It has become an accepted, established institution and is now considered by many to be a "woman's right." Official policy now grants a woman the right to an abortion without any question of its justifiability.

Three contributing factors

Many factors have contributed to the establishment of abortion as an acceptable institution within our society. Three of the most significant are (1) the Supreme Court's *Roe* v. *Wade* decision of 1973, (2) the women's liberation movement's making abortion rights the hallmark of feminism, and (3) the failure of many liberals to affirm their own tradition's essentially "pro-life" values.

The *Roe* v. *Wade* decision said, in effect, that an expectant mother has the legal—and, by implication, moral—right to end the life of her developing unborn during the first six months of its development and, unless a state law intervenes, during the entire pregnancy. This decision has had a powerful educational, as well as legal, result. It teaches that the unborn have essentially no value during the first six months of life and that they may be discarded at will.

In a similar way the majority of feminists (with notable exceptions, such as Feminists for Life of America) have made support of abortion rights the test of faithful adherence to women's liberation. I am a feminist. I believe in the full equality of women and men. In this sense I believe that Jesus was a feminist and that every Christian is called in Christ to recognize and affirm the full humanity and equality of women and men. But I do not believe that any human being has the inherent right to end the life of any other human being at any stage of its development. The fact that it may be justifiable to do so in certain circumstances does not constitute a right to do so in all circumstances.

There is an inconsistency between being both a true feminist and an advocate of abortion rights. True feminism denies the right of any person to possess or control another. Authentic feminists are rightly appalled, for example, by the legal and cultural structure of societies in which wives and daughters are, in effect, the property of their husbands and their fathers. True feminism declares that no one is ever anyone's property and that no one has the right to dominate, let alone destroy, another. True feminism stands for liberation of the oppressed, for protection of the weak and helpless, and for the elimination of all human exploitation. How, then, can feminists maintain that women have "the right" to end the lives of their developing daughters and sons during the first months of life? These developing human beings are the gift of God. They are temporarily at home within their mothers' bodies, but they are not part of her body, nor are they her property. Her womb is their cradle and is designed by their Creator to be a place of nurture and growth and not death. In biblical terms, the mother is the steward, the trustee and not owner, the divinely provided carer as well as carrier of the life of the unborn. This is her sacred trust and responsibility under God.

Imagine a patriarchy in which fathers had "the right" to end the lives of their unborn children. I hope that we are repulsed by the thought of a society in which men had such authority over their wives and their unborn children. There is only one essential difference between the man's situation in that imagined society and the woman's situation in the abortion-rights world of contemporary America, and that is in the fact that the mother is carrying the child.

This is obviously a significant difference. In some circumstances it may mean that it is justifiable to terminate a pregnancy, but it does not mean that she has an inherent right to do so. I believe that to affirm such a legal right is bad law, to affirm such a moral right is poor morality, and to affirm such freedom to destroy the unborn is faulty feminism. It seems ironic to me that after centuries of institutionalized male dominance which gave fathers and husbands the right to control the female property of their wives and daughters, we now have "liberated" women claiming a similar right over their unborn children. It is also ironic that fathers can be required to pay the medical costs of pregnancy and childbirth, and for subsequent child care, while being denied any authority in matters concerning the termination of pregnancy.

I also believe that it is inconsistent for those who claim to be "liberal" to be advocates of "abortion rights." True liberalism affirms the rights of the oppressed and stands for the protection of the weakest members of society, those who cannot defend themselves. Although authentic liberals and authentic conservatives often differ on the means of doing so, both, at their best, are life affirming. At their narrow and legalistic worst, right-wing conservatives have tempted liberals to oppose what they favor, and as a result many of liberal bent are fearful of challenging "abortion rights" lest they be labeled "right-wing fanatics." Classic liberals have always been essentially "pro-life" people; it is tragic that so many contemporary liberals have, in effect, permitted conservatives to claim to be the sole protectors of the unborn. We rightly protest the destruction of baby seals, but how then can so many who speak to save the seals be indifferent to the fate of millions of their own species? To be consistent with their own values, and as Christians to be faithful to their Lord, I believe that both feminists and liberals should affirm the appropriate value of life at all stages of its pre- and postbirth development.

Altered attitudes

A substantial decrease in the number of abortions requires a profound change in attitude away from regarding abortion as a right. Since they helped create current attitudes that accept abortion as a legal and human right, three factors that would have significant influence in altering attitudes would be (1) the repeal of the *Roe v. Wade* decision, or adoption of a constitutional amendment stating that "the right to an abortion is not guaranteed by this constitution"; (2) recognition by feminists of the inconsistency of demanding equality for themselves while denying even a degree of humanity to their unborn children; and (3) the reclaiming by liberals of their authentic, pro-life perspective.

As we now turn to consideration of justifiable versus unjustifiable abortion, we underscore again the basic distinction between granting that there are tragic circumstances in which abortion is justifiable and the current state of affairs in which abortion is an established, institutionalized practice regarded by many as a legal and moral right. The position taken here affirms the former and rejects the latter. It seeks to move the abortion debate out of the realm of right and into the realm of justice, out of established, institutional practice and into that of justifiable, tragic exception.

Justifiable versus unjustifiable abortion

The essential question concerning the justifiability of any particular abortion relates to whether the pregnancy's harm to the woman is sufficient to warrant destruction of the unborn. When the physical life of the mother is threatened, as in cases of ectopic pregnancy, which develops in a fallopian tube, this is true. In pregnancies resulting from rape or incest and others inflicting immense emotional trauma on the expectant mother, as in the case of a very young girl, such warrant may also, though less obviously, be present. If it can be determined that a deformity, such as an anecephalic condition, in which brain development is absent, is so severe that human fulfillment is impossible, an abortion may be warranted. Although it is difficult to be morally definitive in regard to all situations in which abortion may be justifiable, I believe that, apart from the relatively few and often debatable "hard cases," the inherent value of the unborn makes most abortions unjustifiable.

When considering the criteria for justifiable abortion, the stage of the pregnancy is, from one point of view, irrelevant. If human life is fully present from the moment of conception, there is no essential difference between ending that life at one week or six months. Some will even argue that there is really no difference between killing the unborn and taking their lives following birth.

Others of us, who affirm that human life begins at conception, are, nevertheless, open to consider the belief that changes in development during early pregnancy are so significant that they merit change in the value appropriate to the unborn. Some maintain, for example, that it is a mistake to value the first cells of life prior to implantation as highly as the developing unborn after implantation.

Since "brain death" has been regarded as the end of human life, some believe that "brain birth," indicated by electrical activity in the brain detectable about six weeks following conception, is a change of such significance that greater value should be placed on the unborn thereafter and that criteria for justifiable, later abortions should be correspondingly more demanding.

Until recently, many considered the point of viability, when survival is possible outside the womb, as the most significant transition point between conception and birth. Such thinking is basic to the Supreme Court's *Roe* v. *Wade* decision, which, in effect, declares that the unborn have neither rights nor value prior to viability. It has become clear, however, that viability has less to do with the stage of prebirth development than with medical technology which, as noted earlier, may, in effect, make the unborn viable from the earliest days of pregnancy.

Differences: in degree or kind?

Is the difference only in degree, or also in kind, between the developing unborn at five days, five weeks, and five months? There is certainly an immense emotional difference between taking a morning-after pill to prevent implantation and having a midterm abortion, but if human value is constant from the moment of conception, there is no logical difference between termination of pregnancy at one stage or another. However, if preimplantation and prebrain-birth unborn are different in kind, as well as degree, from the reality of later stages of development, less justification for an abortion is required at the earlier stages.

While acknowledging that emotion may have distorted my logic, I must confess some difficulty in totally equating the preimplantation and prebrain-birth unborn with fully differentiated, later development. This does not mean that I favor early abortion, but that I am more deeply troubled over those performed beyond the first weeks of pregnancy. I must also confess that my personal abhorrence of later abortion was increased by the traumatic experience of the unintended, premature birth of our first baby at five months term. She was a little girl who weighed only 1 lb. 13 oz. As I stood by her incubator while she struggled for life the doctor told me that she could not live. If she had been born today in a hospital with a neonatal unit, she might have been saved for a full and joyful life. Without such care she lived for only one hour.

This experience also prompts me to wonder if all who have abortions realize what they are doing. Would they who choose to end the lives of their developing offspring be willing to hold a baby rabbit in their hands and watch it die as they strangled it to death? Yet what is the life of that rabbit in comparison to their own flesh and blood created to live in the image of God?

In asking such questions I do not wish to be unkind or excessively dramatic, but only to be realistic. During the Vietnam War the reality of burning villagers to death with napalm was denied by calling it a "pacification program." In a similar way we deny the reality of abortion by speaking of "termination of pregnancy" rather than the killing or execution of unborn babies. In this chapter I have chosen to refer to "the unborn" rather than "the baby," but I am convinced that the reality in the incubator that day was something more than "the products of conception," or even just "a fetus." She was our little girl. When asked about our children, we often say, "Our first baby was a little girl who was born prematurely and lived only an hour." We would be unrealistic to believe she was something less.

In the next chapter we will consider the temptation to dehumanize, and even demonize, our enemies and will note how Hitler's "final solution" of "the Jewish problem" was preceded by the dehumanization and demonization of the Jews in the minds of Hitler and his cohorts. So, too—though the comparison may seem harsh to some—there is a similar tendency to dehumanize the tiny "enemy" within, whose presence now threatens the serenity, and sometimes the survival, of its mother. Some come close to "demonizing" when they compare the unborn to a ruptured appendix or malignant growth that can be destroyed without a twinge of conscience.

Reverence for mother and child

We are certainly to act with kindness and compassion toward troubled women distressed by unwanted pregnancy. There is much that all who claim to be truly pro-life should do on their behalf, and if such women choose abortion, that care and compassion should not be diminished. To be pro-life is to be pro-woman and to affirm the full humanity and total equality of women and men, but it is not to give women the right to kill their offspring, either before or after birth. No one has such a right to take the life of another.

If there is doubt that the developing unborn is in any measure human, must not the burden of proof rest on those who would deny rather than affirm that humanity? When there is any possibility that an accident victim is alive, we call the doctor and not the mortician. In like manner, if there is even a chance that the unborn is human, must we not at least hesitate to order its destruction? When there is wrestling concerning the rightness or wrongness of a particular abortion, it is evident that the person no longer thinks of abortion as a personal or legal right but has entered into the realm of struggle between the justifiable and unjustifiable in relation to this issue of life and death. Such struggle is often agonizing, but I believe there is no other place where we can take our stand as responsible human beings and as faithful stewards of the Lord of life.

Alternatives to abortion

Much more could be done by way of responsible sex education. It should start young, in the family, in Sunday school and confirmation, as well as young adult programs. It should be a positive presentation of our sexuality as a wonderful gift from a loving God for the expression of love in a relationship of lifelong commitment and for the creation of new life. Our children should learn that pornography is not only anti-woman in its presentation of women as playthings and possessions, but also anti-sex in rejecting the love and commitment that make joyful and lasting sexual fulfillment possible.

Because our children received excellent sex education as part of the standard curriculum in our community's elementary and junior high schools, we affirm such instruction in the public schools. Imperfect sex education is preferable to none at all. In home and church Christians can correct and supplement what is taught in school. We discovered that the school program enabled our children to be amazingly open to discuss sexual matters without embarrassment.

As Christians we believe that premarital chastity is wise as well as virtuous, and that all immorality is in the long run stupid as well as sinful. Sexual sins violate relationships of life and not just rules from an ancient book. Our children should learn that those rules are God's gifts for our good and not hindrances to happiness.

Without minimizing the wisdom and virtue of chastity, we must also recognize that we are living in a sexually permissive society that is unlikely to be persuaded to abandon sexual activity. Therefore, I believe that both church and state should encourage the use of safe contraceptives by all sexually active persons who do not desire parenthood. Development of techniques that enable more precise determination of the woman's time of fertility make "natural family planning" acceptable to many, but this is not the only means of moral contraception. The Roman Catholic church's opposition to "artificial" contraception is based on the erroneous, unbiblical notion that procreation is an essential purpose of all sexual relations and that the possibility of conception must, therefore, be present in every sexual encounter. When sexual relations are understood to be God's gift for the joy and renewal of married life and not just for creating children, it becomes clear that medically safe means of contraception (which prevent conception and not just implantation) are also the gift of God. The Roman Catholic church's witness against abortion would be more persuasive if combined with affirmation of responsible contraception. This change would also make it easier for all Christians to unite in opposition to abortion.

Encouragement to sin?

Some fear that affirming contraception will encourage sinful sexual activity and thus make us accomplices in immorality. I doubt that this is true and believe it is possible to teach chastity and at the same time to stress that a couple should never—yes, *never!*—engage in sexual relations without the use of contraceptives unless they are able and willing to assume the responsibilities of bearing a child.

"In 1980-81, the pregnancy rate for Americans aged 15 to 19 was 96 per 1000, and 45 percent of those pregnancies ended in abortion. In the Netherlands the pregnancy rate was 14 per 1000 with a 37 percent abortion rate."[1] It is reported that Sweden, which is reputed to be a sexually permissive society, has only one-third the number of unwanted pregnancies per capita as does the United States—and correspondingly fewer abortions. These differences are attributed to sex education, easy availability of contraceptives, and encouragement concerning their use. The first step in reducing abortions is to reduce unwanted pregnancies. Therefore, everyone should be taught not only to refrain from illicit sexual relations but also that, should self-control fail, it is simply unthinkable to engage in sexual relations without contraceptive protection.

Elenore Hamilton has suggested that couples should also be taught that there are ways of experiencing sexual fulfillment without intercourse. She believes that a couple should never have intercourse unless they are ready to accept the responsibilities of parenthood and that when this is not the case they should limit their sexual activity to petting, even to the point of mutual sexual satisfaction.[2] Because I question the morality of such activity and doubt that it would be easy for couples to refrain from intercourse after engaging in such physical intimacy, I do not endorse this advice. Nevertheless, I have learned from couples in counseling that some whom I believe to be responsible Christians have used this means of conquering the temptation to have intercourse prior to marriage and also, thereby, avoided the possibility of unwanted pregnancy. Without advocating this practice, I know that all couples in long, intimate relationships must deal with their sexual desires, and believe that limiting sexual activity by commitment to refrain from intercourse is more responsible and more moral than the impulsive, irresponsible sexual behavior that often results in unwanted pregnancy.

When unwanted pregnancy occurs

We should also greatly increase the amount of care and counseling that is available for those with problem pregnancies. Much is already being done by groups like Birthright, and other pro-life counseling centers that affirm reverence for life toward both the mother and her developing, unborn child. Counseling and care centers operating with a Christian perspective face the facts of pregnancy and abortion and seek to convey, gently but firmly, a sense of love for, and stewardship of, the life of the one who may now be regarded as the intruder or even enemy within. The options of keeping the child or placing for adoption are discussed. Responsible counselors do not make decisions for others, but they do inform and clarify so that responsible decisions are possible. Denying or ignoring the facts of what an abortion means for the unborn, in order to make it easier for a woman to have an abortion, is, in my opinion, disrespectful of the woman who has the right to be fully informed, and in the long run injurious to her emotional and spiritual well-being.

With hundreds of qualified couples waiting to adopt, abortions should not be performed to prevent the births of unwanted children. All who know the eagerness of those wishing to become adoptive parents must believe that these babies are often more "wanted" than those of many biological parents. Some reject adoption because of the trauma felt by the mother who gives up the child. This is often a painful emotional experience, but is that pain to be avoided by denying life to the child? If an abortion is less traumatic than surrendering a child to the loving arms of adoptive parents who will joyfully nourish it toward fullness of life, one must wonder if the mother's emotions are really in tune with the realities involved in the adoption and abortion decisions.

As with biological parenthood, there are difficulties in adoptive family life, but none of these problems is "solved" by killing the children. Women with problem pregnancies should not be forced to choose adoption, but they should be presented with the noble option of making this sacrifice of love for their children rather than sacrificing them for either the mother's temporary convenience or to avoid the grief of giving them to other parents to love.

Legal dimensions and dilemmas

Having attempted to wrestle with some of the ethical issues, we now turn to the complex and controversial legal dimensions of the abortion debate. As stated earlier, no judicial or legal action will of itself end all unjustifiable abortions. Whatever happens in this regard, we can expect years of legal and legislative struggle concerning the interpretation and application of the constitution and of national and state statutes concerning abortion.

After more than a decade of legalized abortion on demand, it is also unrealistic to expect that the strict anti-abortion legislation favored by many within the pro-life movement will be easily enforceable. I believe it is possible to provide greater regulation that will result in fewer abortions, but I do not believe it is now possible to prohibit it altogether. To be enactable and enforceable, abortion legislation must be a compromise between what pro-life people desire and pro-choice people oppose.

Advocates of legal and legislative regulation and restriction of abortion should recognize the educational, as well as coercive, function of wise law. One hope in advocating such action is not that it will immediately result in dramatically fewer abortions, but that it will help correct the tragic misconception of abortion as a personal, legal, and moral right and will move the abortion debate into the agonizing arena in which responsible people wrestle with issues related to the justifiable versus unjustifiable taking of life. Unless such a shift occurs, I doubt that there will be many fewer abortions. Wise law would help create greater reverence for the unborn and correspondingly greater opposition to unjustified abortion.

One effective action would be the adoption of a constitutional amendment to declare that the right to an abortion is not guaranteed by the constitution. My personal preference is for a constitutional amendment that says that no one has "the right" to take life at any stage of its pre- or postbirth development and that killing is never permissible except in tragic, exceptional circumstances. Such an amendment would help correct the unwarranted and immoral assumption of a right to kill that underlies the establishment of all institutions of death.

Sin versus crime

The distinction between the ethical and legal dimensions of the abortion debate prompts consideration of the difference between sin and crime. Some sins are crimes, some are not. Some crimes are sins, some are not. Greed and lust are sins, but they are not crimes. It was a crime for Rosa Parks to sit in the front of a segregated bus and for people under Nazi law to save Jews from the death camps, but these were not sins. Sins transgress the will of God and the law of love. Crimes transgress the will of the state and the laws of the land. In a pluralistic society it is neither appropriate nor feasible to make everything we consider sinful to be equally criminal. From a pro-life perspective, it is clearly sinful to have an unjustifiable abortion but it is not equally clear that we should, therefore, write laws making criminals of all women who have such abortions. To do so would probably create such sympathy for the "courageous" women who flaunted the law that it would prove to be both unenforceable and counterproductive.

What then can be reasonably expected of legislative action? If the constitution were reinterpreted or changed to deny the right of abortion, legislation would be possible requiring women seeking abortions to be fully informed through photographs or models about the reality they are thinking of destroying. Some will see this suggestion as designed to create an emotional crisis for the mother in order to make it more difficult for her to choose to abort. But is such legislation more sinister than "truth in lending" laws, demanding that borrowers be told what they are doing? Is it unfair to require that persons considering actions to end the lives of their unborn be fully informed concerning abortion, and of all alternatives, including adoption, that are available?

A legally mandated waiting period of at least three days between application for an abortion and its taking place should also be required. We had three days in which to change our minds following the purchase of a vacuum cleaner and a similar wait following application for a mortgage loan. With laws prescribing time for "second thoughts" concerning such relatively trivial matters, isn't it also equally appropriate to require a period for reflection concerning all decisions related to life and death? When the pregnancy appears advanced beyond the time of brain-birth, law could require an ultrasound photograph to determine the stage of development, and that later abortions not be performed except to protect the life of the mother.

Medical doctors must now report the results of all surgery and are subject to discipline for performing too many unnecessary operations. Excised tissue is examined to discover if it is normal or diseased. Similarly, doctors should also be required to report the medical indications that prompted prescription of abortion, and the stage of development of the fetus. Excised tissue should be examined, and doctors discovered to be regularly performing or prescribing unjustifiable abortions should lose their licenses to practice medicine.

Schools and agencies working with teenagers are required to receive parental permission before permitting field trips, vaccinations, and the like. A teenager's decision to have an abortion involves her parents' grandchild as well as her own baby. Therefore, no abortion should be performed prior to the mother's age of majority without consultation with her parents, and, except when pregnancy threatens the mother's life, parental consent

should be required. On the other hand, since it does not involve
the destruction of their grandchild and can prevent unwanted pregnancy, I believe it should be permissible for doctors to provide
contraceptive information and prescribe contraceptives for teenagers without parental consent.

Practical permissiveness

Although my conviction is that human life begins at conception, I believe that practical legislation may need to reflect
lesser value placed on the unborn prior to implantation. I am
personally opposed to methods of birth control that permit fertilization but prevent implantation. It is, however, doubtful that
laws prohibiting "morning-after" pills and other means of preventing implantation would be wise or enforceable. Legal permissiveness in this regard also avoids the debates concerning cases
of rape, which often divert attention from the central issues.
Health problems related to IUDs will likely diminish their use,
and may require prohibition of these devices.

Practical necessity may also require greater legal permissiveness for abortion between implantation and brain-birth than during
later development. During the first six weeks of pregnancy, abortion might be legal to protect the total health and welfare of the
mother, while those performed following brain-birth would be
permitted only to protect her physical life. Most pro-life people
will oppose such permissiveness, but it may be as much as is
attainable and enforceable.

Laws related to abortion in cases of prenatal deformity and
disability also present an agonizing dilemma. It may be a sin to
have an abortion in cases of diagnosed Down's Syndrome, but
that does not necessarily mean that it should be made a crime.
When there is a significant chance that a child will be deformed,
is it more moral to abort or to permit the birth and then, if the
disability prevents life fulfillment, to kill the child? To ask this
question is not to advocate infanticide, but to note that from the

perspective of justifiable versus unjustifiable taking of life, selective infanticide in tragic circumstances may be ethically preferable to the destruction of many who are normal in order to prevent the birth of some who are severely deformed. Nevertheless, to avoid the slippery slope of legalized infanticide, practical necessity may require legalization of abortions when there is substantial likelihood of serious deformity.

In summary, the position suggested here (1) places no legal restriction prior to implantation, (2) permits legal abortion between implantation and brain-birth when the pregnancy adversely affects the health and welfare of the mother, and (3) permits legal abortion following brain-birth only when *(a)* there is a threat to the physical life of the mother, or *(b)* there is evidence of serious prenatal deformity.

Imposing my morals on others?

Some say, "I don't believe in abortion, but I do not wish to impose my personal morality on others and, therefore, do not believe that we should legally regulate or restrict abortion." There are, however, hundreds of other ways in which we rightly seek to legally restrain others from doing things we consider immoral. We would all be shocked to hear someone say, "I don't believe in child abuse, theft, or murder, but since I do not wish to impose my personal and religious convictions on others, I am opposed to laws against child abuse, theft, and murder." Moral convictions grounded in religious faith are not to be excluded from the political process. I affirm separation of church and state and oppose governmental imposition of religious beliefs and practices, but I also believe that people who consider it sinful to rob banks or torture children are not thereby disqualified from supporting legislation prohibiting such behavior.

Laws rightly protect the weak from the oppression of the strong. Courts and constitutions exist to prevent minorities from being abused by the majority and to secure the rights of one person or group when infringed upon by the free exercise of rights claimed by another. As the old saying goes, "My freedom to swing my arms ends where your nose begins." None of us has the right and freedom to harm someone else. Personal liberty is always limited by social responsibility.

Abortion debates abound with talk about "freedom of choice" and "reproductive freedom." I believe that such freedom exists prior to conception and, therefore, oppose legislation prohibiting the sale and promotion of contraceptives. At conception, however, a new reality comes into being that is distinctly different from the parents who created it and which is neither part of the mother's body nor her private possession. From its beginning, this reality is a tiny universe of mystery coded for growth toward full humanity, and is even at that stage worthy of more reverence than the neighbor's cat. Even when it trespasses in my yard, I do not have the moral or legal right to kill that cat. Nor do we have the right to destroy any of God's born or preborn children, and are, therefore, justified in supporting legislative and judicial action to restrict others from doing so.

The helpless and the voiceless are in greatest danger of suffering unjustly, and are, therefore, in greatest need of legal protection. The developing unborn are among the most vulnerable and most in need of voices and votes raised on their behalf. Some give them value equal to postborn persons from the moment of conception. Others see that value as increasing from conception to full human worth at the time of birth. But, in honest reverence for life, can't we agree that there is no point from conception onward when these beings of divine creation are totally without value? And if this is true, can't we also agree that it is appropriate to at least limit the freedom of those who would kill them?

Regulation, not prohibition

The kind of regulation, but not total prohibition, of abortion advocated here would not make criminals of millions of women. The primary means of enforcement relate to the medical profession and would require doctors who perform abortions to be accountable for their actions under penalty of the suspension or loss of license. Only physicians should be permitted to perform abortions, and others who attempt to make a business of doing so should be subject to criminal penalties. Women who challenge the law by choosing to have late abortions should be treated with compassion, and be subject to civil, but not criminal, penalties. It should also be noted that such civil disobedience, in contrast with that of Gandhi and Martin Luther King Jr., involves an act of violence against another life.

Some believe that any restriction of abortion will drive women to "back-alley butchers" and to self-inflicted "coat hanger" abortions. Dr. Bernard Nathanson, once chairman of the Medical Committee of the National Association for Repeal of Abortion Laws and the director of the world's largest abortion clinic, has been persuaded by developments in the new medical specialty of fetology to become one of abortion's leading opponents. He points out that "technology has eliminated" this argument and made it "wholly invalid and obsolete." He maintains that methods of performing abortion without harm to the mother are now so widely and easily available that "if abortion is ever driven underground again even non-physicians will be able to perform the procedure with remarkable safety" and that "no woman need die if she chooses to abort during the first twelve weeks of pregnancy." Needless to say, in making such statements Nathanson is not encouraging the establishment of underground abortion clinics. He is rather exposing the fallacy of "this most emotional of arguments" that once "swayed me more than any other" to practice abortion.[3]

Global perspectives

Some argue for unrestricted abortion from a global rather than personal perspective. They see humanity drowning in a sea of starving and warring bodies unless reproduction is dramatically reduced, and regard abortion as an essential means of population control. They say, in effect, "If the living are to live, many of the unborn must die."

We can debate the urgency of the population crisis, but it is obvious that a finite planet cannot sustain an infinite population. The real issues, therefore, relate to the most desirable level of population and the means of limiting its growth.

If all means of population control through education and family planning had been fully utilized, a global crisis of intense over-population might provide an argument for abortion. But this is clearly not now the case. As with justifiable warfare, justifable abortion should always be the last resort. Much more can be done to teach responsible contraception and family planning in this country and around the world. When our government refuses to provide financial assistance to family-planning agencies that sometimes encourage abortion, we may enjoy a feeling of righteous purity, but it is doubtful that such restrictions help to prevent abortions. It would be far better to require that none of our funds be used to perform abortions while continuing to support efforts to educate and assist those desiring to practice responsible family planning.

One of the reasons deprived people are so prolific is that they hope to have enough children so that some will survive into adulthood. Therefore, a significant and compassionate way of discouraging excessive reproduction is to provide the health and nutrition that will enable their children to live. When more children survive, the birth rates usually decline.

What we can do now

While promoting legal and judicial change, we should not forget that much more can be done now. States can pass laws regulating abortion during the final trimester. Hospitals can be discouraged from performing unjustifiable abortions. Church and state can educate people concerning the value of the unborn and what is involved in abortion. Although it is legal to smoke cigarettes, our government warns against their use and promotes educational efforts to prevent smoking. In a similar way, would it not be appropriate for the government, even while abortion is legal, to help educate concerning means of avoiding unwanted pregnancy and the realities involved in abortion?

Whatever their views of legislative and judicial action, Christian leaders should stand united in opposition to both irresponsible sexuality and unjustifiable abortion. They should encourage Sunday school, confirmation, and teenage and young adult instruction that emphasizes the goodness of God's gift of sexuality and the wisdom and joy, as well as the morality, of responsible sexual behavior. When unwanted pregnancy occurs, public and private agencies should assure that no one is compelled to have an abortion out of financial necessity.

A consistent, pro-life position also rejects violence against abortion clinics. Bombing abortion clinics will not reduce the number of abortions, and will weaken the witness of those who are truly pro-life in all its dimensions. We do not overcome evil with evil but with good.

Jesus calls us to live with profound reverence for life. With such reverence we affirm the value of human life from conception and claim no right to destroy it. At the same time we face situations in which the taking of life before or following birth may be justifiable, but oppose all tendencies to transform such exceptional necessity into acceptable and established practice. As consistently pro-life people, we grant the occasional necessity of abortion, but we stand against its acceptance as a personal or legal right and seek through compassionate care of those with unwanted pregnancies—through sex education and encouragement of contraception, and through judicial and legal action—to limit the numbers of abortions among us.

5 WAR AND ITS PRO-LIFE ALTERNATIVES

For Christians, the problem of war is twofold: (1) like everyone else, we must face the fact that use of our nuclear defense will, probably, instead of defending us, guarantee our destruction, and (2) as Christians, we must try to bring our attitudes toward war into conformity with the teaching and life of Jesus. The second is a concern with which Christians have wrestled across the centuries; the first is unique to our generation. For the first time, humanity now possesses the capacity for the certain destruction of civilization and the possible extermination of our species. As human beings we seek wisdom to survive and enhance civilization. As Christians we seek to be faithful to Jesus Christ. If all truth is God's truth, and if Jesus is the supreme revelation of God's truth, the ways of wisdom and of faithfulness will meet at the feet of Jesus. The way of wisdom will be the way of Christ, and the way of Christ will be the way of wisdom.

Humanity's challenge
Great evils, including tyrannies of the left and of the right, threaten our freedom and even our survival. Humanity's challenge is to conquer, or at least control, those evils without destroying

the life of the planet. Like a doctor combating cancer, our task is to conquer the cancer without killing the patient. Imagine two doctors consulting concerning a cancer patient. One suggests a specific course of chemotherapy, and the other responds, "I don't think the patient can survive that treatment." Then imagine the first doctor replying, "You are soft on cancer!" Such conversation is obviously absurd. A doctor does not need to love cancer to oppose treatments that kill the patients; nor should everyone who rejects strategies for saving America from Soviet domination by destroying the world be labeled "soft on communism." Even if the Soviet Union were 10 times more evil than its worst critics believe it to be, that would not justify the annihilation of humanity to save us from it. There is no evil within history that justifies our ending history. Humanity is not so sick that global euthanasia is now justifiable.

As the two superpowers struggle to maintain their security and spheres of influence, an ever-present third power is waiting to destroy us all. Its name is *war,* and in its arsenal of nuclear, chemical, and biological weapons is an evil greater than either of the superpowers imagines the other to be. Neither the United States nor the Soviet Union can occupy and control the other. War can destroy them both—and with them, all civilization and possibly all of humanity. Whatever our political perspectives, we must come to realize that the greatest threat to human fulfillment, and to our survival on which that fulfillment depends, is not fascism, communism, or capitalism, but war, which can destroy us all.

About 150 years ago, nearly 40% of all birds in North America were passenger pigeons. Some flocks were estimated to be more than two billion birds! They seemed indestructible. Yet the last passenger pigeon that will ever live on this planet died in a zoo in Cincinnati in 1914. We human beings did that to passenger pigeons! Will we now do it to ourselves? With an escalating arsenal of nuclear, chemical, and biological weapons, it is no joke to ask, "Will there be human beings living on this planet in 2014?

Or 2114? Or 2514?'' We need not quibble about the date! As doomsday devices proliferate around the world, the human prospect becomes increasingly grim. Unless the superpowers take the lead in reversing the arms race, the fate of these cats could be our own:

> There were once two cats of Kilkenny,
> Each thought there was one cat too many,
> So they fought and they fit,
> And they scratched and they bit,
> Till, except for their nails and the tips of their tails,
> Instead of two cats there weren't any.

This grim prospect prompted Freeman Dyson to suggest that the strongest opponents of the nuclear arms race should not be only the physicians and preachers, but "the military," because they should know better than anyone else that these weapons have "ruined war." Retired Admiral Noel Gaylor makes the same point: "One of the most dangerous illusions of our time is to regard nuclear devices as military weapons. They are not military weapons, they are instruments of genocide."

Everything has changed except our thinking

Perhaps Albert Einstein said it best—"The unleashed power of the atom has changed everything save our modes of thinking, and we thus drift toward unparalleled catastrophe."[1] This statement witnesses to the reality of a new era and the tragic unreality of much perception of it. As early as 1946, Einstein had come to believe that "A new type of thinking is essential if mankind is to survive and move toward higher levels," and that to "maintain the threat of military power" was to "cling to old methods in a world which has changed forever."[2]

One 10-megaton bomb has the destructive capacity of 10 million tons of TNT, which is over twice the total of all bombs used in World War II. A train carrying that much TNT would be more than 3000 miles long! Whether unleashed by intention, miscalculation, or accident, the devastation of blast, heat, radiation, disease, and deprivation resulting from even a "little" nuclear war would make the horrors of Hitler's Holocaust pale in comparison. If we exterminate ourselves it will not happen instantaneously but will be the result of the anguishing aftereffects of a war which renders this beautiful planet unfit for human life. By using these demonic instruments of antilife, we can now reverse creation and transform the earth into a habitation for cockroaches.

Everything has changed, but most perceptions remain the same. Many still think of war as army against army and nation against nation. But nuclear war is, as Norman Cousins has said, "war against the whole of which we are a part." It is war against the world, and in Cousins' imagery is compared to inflicting a mortal wound in one's own body or to seeing who can drill the biggest hole in the bottom of the boat in which we are all riding.

In 1862, Abraham Lincoln declared, "The dogmas of the quiet past are inadequate to the stormy present. The occasion is piled high with difficulty, and we must rise to the occasion. As our case is new, so we must think anew and act anew." So too, in relation to nuclear war and global security "we must think anew and act anew" to correct the old, and now deadly, ideas that threaten to drive us all like lemmings to the sea. As we face these realities, I believe that Jesus Christ, the Prince of Peace, is challenging us not only to stop and reverse this irrational, immoral arms race, but also to unite in new thinking and new acting that can lead to the abolition of the institution of war and to the creation of a more just and peaceful world.

Our thinking can change

We rejoice over the abolition of institutions, such as slavery, once considered inherent to human society and even to God's creation. Few preachers now quote the Bible to "prove" that slavery is the will of God, and many Christians now realize that the institutionalized practice of male superiority and feminine subordination is contrary to the way of Christ. We thank God that thinking has changed to affirm the full humanity of women and men of every race.

A similar revolution in Christian thinking is long overdue in relation to our understanding of war. If humanity survives to look back on centuries of war making, I believe that Christians will then regard our support of war as we now regard earlier support of slavery. It will then be clear that one of Christianity's greatest failures (perhaps of even more tragic consequence than its support of slavery and sexism) was its acceptance, and frequent blessing, of war as an institution for the resolution of human conflict.

It is well to remember that Christians did not always bless war making. For the first 300 years of Christian history, the majority of Christians were clearly opposed to war. Some may have served in police forces, but most refused to participate in warfare. With the development of Constantinian Christianity and the justifiable-war theories, opposition to war gave way to almost universal acceptance of Christian participation in whatever wars their leaders called them to fight. For centuries, Christians fought pagans and each other without being challenged concerning conscience or conformity to the way of Jesus. Most Christians have likened battle sacrifices to the sufferings of Christ, and have failed to recognize the vital distinction made by Harry Emerson Fosdick:

Christendom marches into war after war, taking Christ along on both sides of the battle line, and the Christians sing with exalted spirit, "As he died to make men holy, let us die to make men free." In the interest of intellectual clarity, if nothing else, I should like to set the record straight. That typical war song of Christendom, dragging Christ to battle, needs to have the sentimentality squeezed out of it. Realistically it must read like this: As he died to make men holy, let us *kill* to make men free. Alas, that spoils the song. We cannot sing it that way. We cannot easily fit Jesus into it. We can imagine him dying to make men free. Can we imagine him killing to make men free? That is to say, it is sheer intellectual befuddlement to lump all self-sacrifice together and baptize it *en masse* in the name of Christ. All self-sacrifice does not mean the same thing. *Christ sacrificed himself rather than use violence: He did not sacrifice himself in using violence.*[3]

The horror of two world wars, the carnage of dozens of regional conflicts, and the development of doomsday devices that threaten to destroy everything they are designed to defend have prompted many to question the justifiability of modern warfare. After centuries of neglect, the criteria for justifiable participation in war are being reconsidered and reapplied.

Justifiable versus unjustifiable warfare

As we note some of the criteria common to most of the just/unjust-war theories, remember that a justifiable war must pass *all* these tests:

1. Justifiable war had to be a last resort. If not preceded by negotiation and all attempts to compromise, it was not justified.
2. It required a just cause such as self defense. Wars fought for conquest, wealth, and vengeance were unjustified.
3. There had to be reasonable hope of success, which meant both military victory and attainment of the just cause for which the war was fought.
4. The prospective good to be attained had clearly to outweigh the suffering inflicted by the war. It was sinful to participate in a war that did more harm than good.
5. A just war required a right attitude. A Christian was to love the enemy and never fight with hatred, vengeance, or in retaliation.
6. A just war had to be declared by legitimate authority, and the enemy informed of conditions to be met to avoid the conflict.
7. Just war required just conduct. Civilians and prisoners of war were to be protected. Torturous weapons were not to

be used. Oppression and humiliation of the conquered were
forbidden.

A significant corollary to these criteria is that a war cannot be
justified on both sides. Therefore, Christians should never fight
each other. Participation on at least one side is always unjustifiable.

Had these criteria been heeded, Christians could not have participated in many of the wars they were commanded to fight, nor
could their Christian leaders justifiably have ordered them to do
so. If most Christians had refused to fight in unjustifiable wars,
it seems certain that there would have been many more martyrs
and many fewer wars.

Apply these criteria to war with doomsday devices, napalm,
cluster bombs, and flamethrowers. Note the spirit of hatred and
vengeance that captures a nation in times of cold and hot warfare.
Remember that "instant, massive retaliation" is the basic threat
sustaining the deterrence doctrine of both superpowers. It is then
obvious that there are few, if any, circumstances in which a Christian can in good conscience participate in or support modern
warfare. Facing this reality, many Christians who supported the
war against Hitler have become "nuclear pacifists." Others have
renounced war and war making altogether. Through honest application of the criteria for justifiable war, they have arrived at a
position close to some forms of Christian pacifism.

Is bomb building sinful?

If it is a sin to use such instruments of mass destruction,
is it also a sin to build, deploy, and threaten their use? With 20/
20 hindsight it is easy for us to see that German Christians should
have refused to help build the Nazi death camps, but with silent
acquiescence we support the building of weapons that can kill
more people in minutes than Hitler's war and "final solution"
killed in a decade. There is, in effect, another Auschwitz or
Dachau in every missile warhead.

The Roman Catholic bishops renounce the use of such weapons, but acknowledge that they may be *temporarily* justifiable as a deterrent during the transition to a more moral security system. Such thinking reflects the ambiguity of our sinful world, but it may be heard as continued blessing for their further deployment and threatened use. Therefore, it may be time for Christians of the world to unite in a common confession comparable to the Confessing Church's Barmen Declaration in 1934, which stood against immoral, idolatrous obedience to Hitler. Such a contemporary declaration would confess willingness to live without the "protection" of devices of mass destruction and would oppose their production, possession, and threatened, as well as actual, use.

Can Christians serve in the military?

From the perspective of just/unjust-war theory, this question must be answered in the affirmative. Christians can enter the military with willingness to participate in a justifiable war, but this does not mean that they must fight in wars they believe to be unjust. In faithfulness to Christ and conscience, a Christian must retain the option of refusing to participate in such conflicts. Selective conscientious objection to participation in particular wars is inherent in just/unjust-war doctrine. This is also the teaching of the *Augsburg Confession* and of the New Testament, from which it quotes in stating, "Christians are obliged to be subject to civil authority and to obey its commands and laws in all that can be done without sin. But when commands of the civil authority cannot be obeyed without sin, we must obey God rather than men (Acts 5:29)" (*Augsburg Confession* Article 16; Tappert edition). The secular authority of the Nuremburg Court similarly declared that crimes against humanity cannot be justified on the grounds of obedience to governmental authority.

Military chaplains have a special responsibility to confront and educate our service men and women in this regard. Questions concerning the justifiability of war in general, of nuclear war, of a particular war, and of specific weapons systems should be faced and discussed. A missile silo soldier should not postpone thinking about the morality of launching that missile until receiving the order to fire. The moral issues should be confronted in detail and depth long before that fateful moment, and our chaplains should lead the discussion. Pastors in military service should be free to preach against participation in all forms of unjust war making, and if prevented from doing so should protest and, if need be, resign. Blind obedience to human authority in the military or anywhere else is not patriotism but idolatry, to be rejected in principle and practice.

For committed Christians, the basic question is not, "Can I sometimes *refuse* to participate in war and war making?" but, "Can I *continue to support* the institution of war, which now threatens the life of the planet?" Even without having studied historic Christian just/unjust-war theory, many realize that no war is justified that results in more harm than good and there is no evil on earth that justifies the incineration and radiation of the human race. They see such folly as comparable to curing our headaches by cutting off our heads. Without being naive concerning the Soviet or any other threat, they understand that such a "defense" is neither rational nor moral. Long ago a warrior in Israel was asked: "Must the sword destroy to the utmost? Do you not know that afterward there will be bitterness? How much longer will you refrain from ordering the people to stop the pursuit of their brothers?" (2 Sam. 2:26 NAB). These questions are now addressed to all the war makers of the world.

Unresolved moral problems

We Christians need not be experts in military strategy to recognize that there are unresolved moral problems at the heart of both the deterrence and counterforce doctrines. Threatening "massive assured destruction" may deter an aggressor, but if it fails, there is no justification for retaliation that would only make everything worse. We might deter murder by threatening to kill the family and friends of every murderer, but once a murder occurred it would be barbaric to do so. We are rightly appalled when terrorists threaten to kill innocent persons unless their demands are met. The policy of deterrence depends on threatened murder on such a grand scale that we do not even think of it as terrorism.

Imagine feuding neighbors who were deterring each other's aggression by threatening to explode thousands of sticks of dynamite planted in each other's basements. If discovered, they would be immediately arrested and subjected to psychiatric examination. No community would tolerate such a threat to the neighborhood. Yet when the superpowers behave in similar fashion and threaten the survival of all humanity, many continue to call it "defense" and "national security" instead of labeling it the insanity it truly is.

There may be some comfort in the fact that deterrence has helped prevent war between the superpowers, but this is no reason to be confident of its continued success. In response to such confidence, someone replied: "My grandmother wasn't sick until the day she died," and another likened it to the comment of a person who had fallen from an 80th floor window who was heard to say while passing the 40th floor, "Everything is OK so far." In spite of past success, there may be disaster ahead. One miscalculation could destroy us all. Many factors, other than threat of nuclear annihilation, have also served to prevent war between the superpowers. Being aware, for example, of the chronic indigestion that would follow an attempt to gobble up Western Europe, it is doubtful that the Kremlin would launch such an adventure, even in the absence of the nuclear deterrent.

Although deterrence is our official policy, the deployment of counterforce weapons targeted against missile sites and military installations is convincing evidence that we are shifting to a war-fighting, first-strike strategy. Counterforce weapons are useless for retaliation. There is no sense in attacking an empty missile silo. These are first-strike weapons that must be launched in a surprise attack in order to destroy the enemy's arsenal before it can be fired against us. Targeting military sites may seem more moral than targeting population centers, but this is a deception. Such a surprise strike would result in the "incidental" killing of millions of innocent people, without our having been attacked ourselves.

The development of counterforce weapons also necessitates a hair-trigger alert on both sides, and greatly increases the likelihood of accidental war. It is difficult to imagine any rational motive for attacking missile sites other than to prevent an attack by them. With only minutes between the perception of such an attack and the time of response, there will be no opportunity for either side to consult with anyone. Computers will decide the fate of the earth! From a Christian perspective such trust in the false god of the supercomputer is idolatry and may prove to be humanity's ultimate folly. When someone says, "You can't trust the Russians," we should remember that we are trusting them and their computers every moment of every day to refrain from blowing us off the face of the earth.

To escape the moral and security dilemmas inherent in both the deterrence and counterforce strategies, a new "Strategic Defense Initiative" has been advocated and funded for research development. This "Star Wars" proposal envisions a system of satellite weapons that would destroy attacking missiles. Apart from being well-intended, popular (who can be against defense?), and certain to further enrich the military-industrial-scientific complex, there are many problems with this proposal. (1) Even if successful, it will only defend against intercontinental ballistic missiles, and offers no defense against cruise missiles and all other delivery systems. (2) It will be easy to attack and subvert by use of decoys and dummy missiles. (3) It must work perfectly without having been tested in operation. A 1% failure would be a 100% disaster. (4) It will be immensely expensive. Estimates for full deployment reach to a trillion dollars and beyond. (5) It will guarantee further escalation of the arms race. Anti-missiles will necessitate anti-anti-missile weapons; then anti-anti-anti missile weapons, etc. etc. Defensive systems will prompt increased offensive systems. (6) By encouraging belief in a technological fix, attention is diverted from the political and human relations issues that are central to global security. Like misplaced trust in the supercomputer, this is idolatry of technology. (7) SDI is perceived by the Soviet Union as an offensive, rather than defensive, shield, intended to protect the U.S. from Soviet missiles that have survived our preemptive first strike. This is the chief reason for Soviet opposition to the proposal and the factor that gives it some value as a bargaining chip in negotiations. Soviet opposition should not be taken as proof that "Star Wars" will be good for them and bad for us—in the long run it will be bad for everybody.

A crime against humanity

Even if humanity can be spared the horror of nuclear war, the escalating arms race is in itself a crime against humanity. The global expenditure of more than two billion dollars a day for military purposes—to the neglect of persons who are ill who could be healed and hungry people who could be fed—results every day in the death and deprivation of thousands of God's children. "The arms race kills even without war."[4] Therefore, we must ask not only, "Is nuclear war justifiable?" but also, "Is the arms race itself justifiable?" Can we go on for decades draining away riches of mind and money to create more and more effective means of death while millions of God's suffering children are deprived of the health and hope these resources could provide? In the name of Christ and of human rationality, we must cease this warring madness and find a better way.

What else can we do?

Many agree that nuclear war is unjustifiable and that the arms race is a crime against humanity, but they raise the plaintive cry, "What else can we do? This is a wicked world. Enemies threaten our destruction. We, therefore, have no alternative but to build more weapons to keep the peace and preserve our freedom." This, I believe, is how most of us live—vaguely aware of the horrible prospect of nuclear war and of the horrendous waste of the arms race—but at the same time feeling helpless to do anything about it. The problem is compounded by the fact that the danger is not immediately visible. Birds are still singing and our children are at play. We go about our work and fill our lives with activities that successfully, and perhaps fatally, crowd out awareness of the shadow of nuclear death under which we live each day. If told that there was one chance in a thousand that our furnace might explode, every one of us would immediately move out, order repairs, and refuse to return until they were completed. The same kind of decisive action is required *now* to prevent anyone from blowing up the planetary house in which we are all living.

When we feel helpless and hopeless, our feelings deceive us. Fatalistic hopelessness and helplessness is a denial of both our faith and rationality. We need not follow the example of the pathetic people of Jonestown who drank from the poison vats and poisoned their children. There are alternatives to violence. The threat of war is not a plague from outer space. We created this monstrous machine and we can dismantle it.

In 1910 William James wrote *The Moral Equivalent of War*, in which he yearned for a challenge to humanity as compelling of courageous action as the trumpet's call to war. We now face such a challenge. Our task is twofold: (1) to abolish the institution of war, and (2) *at the same time*, to create alternative institutions that are effective, moral, functional substitutes for war.

There will always be conflict in a sinful world. Individuals and groups will rise up against each other. This is what the Bible means when it speaks of "wars and rumors of wars" existing until the end of time (Mark 13:7). But there is nothing in the

Bible that commands or necessitates the present institution of war. Sydney J. Harris makes this vital distinction:

> War is not eternal. . . . "You'll always have war" is one of the most stupid and thoughtless statements a person could make. . . . What such a person really is saying is that you'll always have aggression and hostility and conflict among people. There is no question of that . . . . But war is a very different matter. War is a social institution, and like any institution it can be abolished— as cannibalism was abolished, as slavery was abolished—if enough of us want to.[5]

The abolition of war will be exceedingly difficult and costly, but it is not impossible. It will demand courage, commitment, and sacrifice comparable to those of war. Our challenge is to think and act in new ways to enable a "postwar" era, in which conflicts are resolved and oppressors overcome by nonviolent means.

Humanity is unlikely to abandon war making until there are functional alternatives to war. If these do not exist, we can create them. In fact, if humanity is to survive and thrive, we *must* create them. The abolition of the institution of war is not a luxury; it is a necessity. We will abolish war or war will abolish us.

Where can we find these alternatives? I believe that they are revealed in the Bible and especially in the teaching and example of Jesus. Here we discover what might be called "the Jesus alternatives" to violence and war. In this chapter we will focus on four alternatives to war proclaimed by the Prince of Peace: (1) peace through justice, (2) peace through reconciliation, (3) peace through global security, and (4) peace through the way of the cross. To visualize their interrelatedness, imagine a tower built on a solid foundation. Justice is the foundation; reconciliation, global security, and the way of the cross are the walls of the tower of peace. If any part is missing, a storm or tremor could cause it to fall. When solidly constructed together these four can provide a lasting structure of peace.

Peace through Justice

"Justice," said Isaiah, "will bring about peace; right will produce calm and security" (Isa. 32:17 NAB). "If you want peace," said Pope Paul VI, "work for justice." Jesus came to "proclaim justice to the nations" (Matt. 12:18 NIV) and said "Woe to" those who "neglected the weightier matters of the law" including "justice" (Matt. 23:23). When we recall all that Jesus taught about love, including "love your enemies" (Luke 6:27), it is well to remember that "justice," as Joseph Sittler has said, "is love operating at a distance."

Justice means respect for the dignity and equality of opportunity of every person. The creation of justice requires opposition to racism, sexism, ageism, self-righteous tribalism and nationalism, and every form of political, cultural, religious, and economic oppression. These and all other forms of human exploitation constitute injustice that often leads to violence and war. Working toward the elimination of injustice in a sinful world is an immensely difficult and endless task requiring continued commitment of mind, muscle, and money comparable to full-scale warfare.

The Christian church has been better at providing charity than creating justice. We have cared for the oppressed, but have often failed to confront the oppressor. Tolerance of injustice, and even unholy alliances with exploiters of the people, are among the great sins of Christian history that have often contributed to tyranny and war. An evangelical pastor in the Soviet Union told us that, "If the Christian church at the time of the Czars had stood for justice and fullness of life for all the people there would not have been a Communist revolution." Historians may debate that point, but it seems certain that lasting peace cannot be built on injustice, and that many revolutions, past and present, are primarily the result of internal oppression, not foreign intervention.

When considering injustice it is well to begin with confession of our own sins and not just the sins of others. We are quick to denounce the oppression of our enemies, but are less ready to confess the injustice of our friends. It is especially difficult for us to see, and then to confess, that we ourselves are acting unjustly. To illustrate our blindness, I recall a conversation between an American seminary professor and an African pastor. Noting certain African marriage customs different from those of Christians in America, the professor asked, "How can you call yourselves Christians when you tolerate these practices?" To which the African pastor replied, "How can you call yourselves Christians, while you are so attached to money and possessions, so self-indulgent in providing luxuries for yourselves and so limited in providing necessities for others?" Each may have been correct in challenging the other.

We rejoice in our affluence and do not intend to hurt anyone by enjoying the things we possess. But our greedy, wasteful over-consumption of the world's resources may be contributing to the sufferings of millions who live around us and who will live after us. Our most grievous failures may be in sins of omission—not in the evil we have done but in the good left undone. By having failed to do more to help the hungry, not only to eat but to produce food for themselves, we may even be guilty of murder—not by intention, but by indifference; not by action, but by inaction.

We are strongly tempted to live by the so-called lifeboat ethic, which asserts that the wealthy are justified in staying alive while we let others suffer and die. There is much self-righteous arrogance in this perspective. Might not some of the perishing be more worthy of life than ourselves? Shouldn't some of us offer to exchange places with them? A latent racism also permeates such thinking. Would we white Anglo-Saxons be as complacent about the suffering and starvation of our European relatives, and as ready to rationalize their deaths, as we are to apply the lifeboat ethic to African and Asian people? While creativity and compassion remain among us it is utterly unjustifiable to solve the unknown and probably manageable problems of the next generation by letting suffering people die today. If such attitudes prevail among the rich and powerful, no amount of weapons will keep them safe, nor will peace long prevail in a world half-stuffed and half-starved. Our problem may be that we have too much to defend, and the beginning of a solution would be to see our wants as less important than others' needs.

When enforced by a tyrannical communist government, the principle "from each according to ability; to each according to need" can result in an oppressive and stifling economic and political system. But when practiced voluntarily by persons captured by the love of Christ, that principle, as stated in texts such as Acts 2:43-47 and 4:32-35, expresses the ultimate in Christian stewardship and prompts each of us to ask, "What right have I to luxuries when others lack the necessities of life?"

It is doubtful that the Christian message will be heard with meaning by the world's suffering people unless those who proclaim it demonstrate commitment to justice for all and not just to prosperity and power for themselves. Early in the last century, Charles Finney declared that a significant hindrance to revival was the church's frequent failure to stand against the abomination of slavery. Similarly, we can hardly expect oppressed people to hear our story of God's love in Jesus Christ while we live in easy toleration of injustice from which they suffer, and in support of the wasteful militarism that drains the lifeblood from efforts to create a more just society. When we realize that global military spending consumes more than two billion dollars a day, it is obvious that the resources for building a more just world are available. Our challenge is to redirect them from destruction to construction, from death to life.

To acknowledge our own sins is not to excuse others. We have no monopoly on either vice or virtue. Having confessed our sins, we are also to confront the sins of others. When we observe injustice, whether practiced by friends or foes, we should do all in our power to confront and correct it.

Facing and admitting our contribution to the world's injustice does not prove that our motives are evil. Most of our intentions are noble—we wish freedom and prosperity for all God's children. But it is not enough to mean well. Much of the world's injustice has been committed by well-intentioned people seeking to preserve the values of the status quo, throw off the yoke of an oppressor, right a great wrong, or keep "dangerous" people from taking over the world. While judging others by their actions, perpetrators of injustice tend to judge themselves by their motives. They claim to be seeking the best for their people and for the world, but at the same time act in ways that bring misery to others and often, in the long run, even to themselves.

Harry Emerson Fosdick told of a man who boarded a bus intending to go to Detroit. After a long journey he discovered that he was not in Detroit but in Kansas City. He had caught the wrong bus! He knew where he wanted to go, but in spite of his good intentions he traveled a road to a different destination. That story illustrates the cause of much of our personal and corporate misery. We have good goals but we travel roads that lead somewhere else. While intending prosperity and peace, governments often follow policies that lead to depression and war. As people committed to "liberty and justice for all" we need to consider the consequences of our actions and not just the nobility of our good intentions.

When we care about people, we care about everything that affects their lives, and that means that we must be concerned about and be involved in the political process. No political party or perspective is perfect, but that is not an excuse for abandoning politics to others. As members of a democratic society that often elects its representatives by a majority of a minority who choose to vote, we probably get better leaders than we deserve. We do well to remember the old saying that "for evil to succeed it is only necessary for good people to do nothing."

Injustice is a fundamental, but not the only, cause of war. Fear, greed, and pride may motivate free and affluent societies to distrust and destroy each other. Commitment to justice is necessary, but insufficient, to create lasting peace. Justice is the foundation of the tower of peace. We will now consider the rest of the structure.

PEACE THROUGH RECONCILIATION

Worship is a high point of Christian life, but when alienation exists Jesus says, "leave your gift there before the altar and go; first be reconciled to your brother" (Matt. 5:23). When the prospect of war is futile, the wise king "sends an embassy and asks terms of peace" (Luke 14:31-32). When Jesus drew near to Jerusalem "and saw the city he wept over it, saying 'Would that even today you knew the things that make for peace!' " (Luke 19:41-42). We are called to be "peacemakers" (Matt. 5:9) and not just peacekeepers or peace lovers. In Christ we have been given "the ministry of reconciliation" (2 Cor. 5:18).

When some complained that Soviet citizens had been invited to an adult forum in our church, Professor Ray Anderson of Augsburg College responded by reminding us all that "We Christians are in the reconciliation business." We are not experts in military strategy but as disciples of Jesus we are to specialize in the nonviolent resolution of conflict, and to support peaceful reconciliation whenever possible.

Although we affirm that no war should ever be fought except as a last resort, it becomes evident when we compare the time and money spent on learning war with that spent on learning reconciliation and negotiation, that we are doing much more to teach war making than peacemaking. In their pastoral letter on peace, the Roman Catholic bishops suggest that we devote one-tenth of one percent of current military spending to teaching the arts of reconciliation and negotiation. One-tenth of one percent seems next to nothing. Yet, that tiny fraction of current American military spending would provide more than 300 million dollars a year! Imagine a National Academy of Peace and Conflict Resolution funded with that money. Think of thousands of students learning the arts of reconciliation and then going out to practice and teach them in every area of human conflict. Then consider what could be done with reallocation of one percent, or five percent, or ten percent of military money for the purposes of not only learning the arts of reconciliation but also for correcting some of the injustice that we have noted to be at the root of war.

We have been given a vision of a time when nations "shall beat their swords into plowshares, and . . . neither shall they learn war anymore" (Isa. 2:4), but we pour millions into our military academies and war colleges and billions more into training all who serve in the military and work on military projects. We devote next to nothing in either money or brain power to train for reconciliation. Is it any wonder that we are more skilled at making war than at making peace?

There are risks in negotiation, but they pale in comparison to the dangers of continued arms escalation. We need to remember Pearl Harbor and to avoid the kind of appeasement associated with Chamberlain at Munich, but we also need to remember the story of Rehoboam, told in 1 Kings 12:1-20, whose tragic error was arrogance of power and unwillingness to compromise. Reconciliation rather than confrontation holds promise of peace based on mutual self-interest, respect, and understanding, rather than on endless threat of terror.

Once upon a time a nation's security was enhanced by increasing the insecurity of its neighbors. The most feared was also the most secure. This is no longer true among nuclearized nations. The more one country frightens the other, the more insecure they both become. Threats and scare tactics may even panic the enemy into launching the very attack a country is trying to avoid. To be secure, nuclear powers must act in ways that enhance rather than diminish their adversary's sense of security.

A great temptation

In times of tribal conflict we are tempted to dehumanize and even demonize our enemies. Building the gas chambers of Hitler's "final solution" to "the Jewish problem" was preceded by dehumanizing and demonizing the Jews in the mind of Hitler and his cohorts. After being designated less than human, and even as the incarnation of everything evil, it seemed only natural and right—from this sick and sinful perspective—that the Jews be exterminated. When we regard our enemies as "the focus of evil in the world," we are tempted to create and use a similar "final solution" worse than Hitler could have imagined. When the adversary is like-minded toward us, a situation of mutual dehumanization and demonization creates fear and hostility that must be overcome if peace is to prevail.

A dangerous form of dehumanization is expressed in Stalin's statement that "one death is a sorrow, ten deaths is a tragedy, a million deaths is a statistic." In calculating the imagined casualties in nuclear war, we are easily captured by this kind of statistical immorality. We need to know that there are human beings with names and faces among our adversaries. Perhaps the families of Soviet military and political leaders should live in the United States and the families of United States' leaders in the Soviet Union. Strategists who consider "limited" nuclear war with only 10-20 million deaths to be "winnable" might experience a rebirth of reverence for life if they knew their loved ones were among those millions.

Roger Fisher, director of the Harvard Negotiation Project, suggests a satirical solution to this statistical dehumanization. He recommends that the code necessary to start a nuclear war no longer be carried in a briefcase by a military officer who accompanies the President, but that instead;

Put that needed code number in a little capsule and then implant that capsule next to the heart of a volunteer. The volunteer would then carry with him a big, heavy butcher knife as he accompanied the President. If ever the President wanted to fire nuclear weapons, the only way he could do so would be for him, first, with his own hands, to kill one human being. The President says, "George, I'm sorry, but tens of millions must die." He has to look at someone and realize what death is—what an innocent death is. Blood on the White House carpet. It's reality brought home.

When I suggested this to friends in the Pentagon they said, "My God, that's terrible. Having to kill someone would distort the President's judgment. He might never push the button."[6]

That someone could perceive that having to kill one person might "distort the President's judgment" so that he might refrain from killing millions witnesses to the unreality, and immorality, of those who coolly calculate the number of "acceptable" casualties in a nuclear war. Christlike reverence for life rejects the barbarity of those who are willing to do technologically and at a distance what only the most depraved murderers can do face to face.

A serious solution to our demonizing misconceptions involves exchanges that would enable us to meet as human beings. We need to learn that there are human beings, and not devils, living in the Soviet Union, and they need to learn the same about us. What might happen if we and the U.S.S.R. were to develop cultural and educational exchanges that enabled 100,000 citizens annually to spend a year in the other country? We would discover common hopes, fears, and aspirations. We would learn that we all treasure the joys of family life, love our children, and want the best for them. Many would be surprised to share the common heritage of our Christian faith. For a tiny fraction of the cost of military spending, we would deepen understanding, diminish fears, and build the basis of lasting, peaceful coexistence.

Problems in human relations

Roger Fisher provides a vivid illustration of the fact that international conflicts are not just problems of military balance, but of human relationships. He asks us to imagine an angry couple throwing dishes at each other. Some of military mentality would, he suggests, call for a "crockery expert" to help them solve their marital problems. This "ceramics specialist" would assess the "throw weight" of all their dishes and help each of them acquire enough cups, plates, and saucers to match the other's arsenal, and then there would be peace in the family. The absurdity of such a "solution" is obvious. This is a human relations and not just a crockery problem. These people need reconciliation. They need a marriage counselor, not a "crockery expert."

Similarly, the world's great need is not for more military specialists, but for experts in the arts of reconciliation and negotiation. Neither a "Star Wars" defense nor any other technological fix can ultimately resolve any of humanity's basic problems. Peace is neither the absence of conflict nor the presence of an impenetrable wall or shield. Peace is the nonviolent, dare we even say "Christian," resolution of conflict. There will always be conflict in a sinful world, but the current system of war making will not exist forever. Being carnivores does not require us to be cannibals; being sinful does not compel us to be murderers or warriors. Nearly all human conflicts are resolved peacefully through conversation, negotiation, and arbitration. No civilized country permits its citizens to solve their problems by killing each other. Violence is the exception, not the rule, except as the ultimate sanction in international relations. We must learn to resolve international problems by talking, not killing, as we do in every other arena of life. We must abolish war, or war, like a cancer that destroys itself by killing its host, will end war by ending humanity. A wise cynic has observed that the institution of war making "will be abolished either before or after the next world war!"

Annual summit conferences

Prospects for reconciliation would be greatly improved if the United States and the Soviet Union would hold annual summit conferences regardless of the state of tension between them. Any neutral site would be suitable for this purpose but none would be better than Hiroshima or Nagasaki. Meeting there would help the adversaries concentrate on solving humanity's most pressing problem, rather than on confronting each other. After agreeing to reduce their own arsenals, they should invite all other nuclear powers to join in multinational disarmament. Then the countries without nuclear weapons could be more reasonably persuaded to accept an enforceable nonproliferation treaty to prevent the further militarization of the planet with doomsday weapons.

Unilateral steps toward peace

Both the United States and the Soviet Union could take concrete steps to facilitate negotiation. There would be little risk, for example, for either superpower to suspend testing and deployment of new weapons for a period of time while challenging the other to respond in kind. The partial test ban treaty was initiated in this way. President Kennedy unilaterally announced that the United States would no longer test nuclear weapons in the atmosphere. The Soviet Union reciprocated, and neither has since conducted an atmospheric test. It is tragic that a comprehensive test ban treaty prohibiting all testing of nuclear devices and their delivery systems was not adopted long ago. Since no nation would dare rely on untested weapons, such a ban, which is verifiable, would have prevented most escalation of the arms race.

Both superpowers have taken many unilateral steps to escalate the arms race. Each should now take courageous unilateral first steps, always inviting reciprocal response, to reduce our common peril. While such a process of unilateral initiation and response is under way, negotiations should continue in order to make temporary achievements permanent through treaty agreements.

Sense of history and sense of sin

The history of nations tells of friends becoming enemies and enemies friends. International conflicts are temporary phenomena. A few years ago we were locked in mortal struggle with German and Japanese enemies who are now among our best friends. Then the Soviets were an ally; now they are an enemy. Some said that we had to fight in Vietnam in order to keep from fighting the Chinese on the beaches of California. Now the Chinese, though still Communist, appear to be our friends. With even a slight sense of history, it appears irrational and immoral for temporary enemies to threaten each other with weapons that can do permanent harm to the entire human family.

When a sense of history is combined with a sense of our own sinfulness, it also becomes obvious that the annihilation of our "enemies" is an abhorrent solution to any international problem. Immense self-righteousness is required to will or perform such a deed. When Jesus declared, "Let him who is without sin among you be the first to throw a stone at her," the would-be executioners had enough character to walk away "one by one, beginning with the eldest" (John 8:7-9). Today, those words confront all the principalities and powers, saying, in effect, "Let the nation without sin cast the first nuclear weapon." Commitment to Christ and common sense now combine in calling us to renounce violence and war and to affirm "the ministry of reconciliation" (2 Cor. 5:18).

That ministry stands in the context of newness in Christ. 2 Corinthians 5:17 is usually understood to say that every person in Christ is "a new creation," but it can also be translated, "When anyone is united to Christ, there is a new world; the old order has gone, and a new order has already begun" (2 Cor. 5:17 NEB). In Christ we are new persons, and there is also "a new world." In Christ we love not only our neighbors but also our enemies. We work for the good of all, including those who persecute us. In Christ we "destroy" our adversaries by reconciliation, not annihilation. We get rid of our enemies, as Lincoln said, by making them our friends.

Peace through reconciliation is one wall in the house of peace. Reconciliation is necessary, but it cannot stand alone. Peace through reconciliation needs the support of peace through global security and peace through the way of the cross.

PEACE THROUGH GLOBAL SECURITY

E. Stanley Jones gave memorable expression to the unity of the global Christian family: "Every person who belongs to Christ belongs to every person who belongs to Christ." In Christ we are members not only of a race, tribe, or nation, but of the worldwide family of the people of God, and are citizens not only of the United States but of all humanity. Global citizenship does not exclude proper national patriotism and love of country, but it does place them in planetary perspective. Our supreme allegiance is not to Uncle Sam, but to Jesus Christ. Total subservience to the will of any nation is not patriotism, but idolatry. Christians with global allegiance can say with Jean Monnet, "I love my country too much to be a nationalist." We are challenged in Christ to be among the vanguard of a new, global community.

For too long, "the dominant intelligence . . . has been trained on tribal business rather than on the operation of human society as a whole." There is therefore "the need for a new consciousness . . . that can take into account the condition of the species rather than only the condition of any of its subdivisions."[7] These thoughts from Norman Cousins remind us that just as our loyalty to the city and state is superseded by loyalty to the nation, so loyalty to the nation must now be superseded by loyalty to humanity. Birth of a new sense of global perspective is essential to counter the narrow and sometimes idolatrous nationalism that fuels the arms race. "War today," says M. Scott Peck, "is at least as much a matter of national pride as of racial pride. What we call nationalism is more frequently a malignant national narcissism. . . . It is our national narcissism . . . that clings to our outmoded notions of sovereignty and prevents the development of effective international peacekeeping machinery."[8] If humanity is to survive and move toward greater fulfillment, the "territorial morality" that labels people murderers when they kill a neighbor across the street and heroes when they kill an enemy across the border must be replaced by a new sense of "global morality" that makes it equally criminal to settle international as well as internal disputes by killing one another. It is especially heinous for Christians to go to war against each other. A poster on my office wall makes, "A modest proposal for peace—that the Christians of the world stop killing each other."

From the perspective of planetary citizenship, all war is civil war. No governmental system can prevent all strife. We can only imagine, however, the number of wars that would have been fought on this continent if we had continued as separate colonies with authority to raise armies to fight each other, rather than creating the federation of the United States of America. There is intense, sporting rivalry between the states, but it is almost unthinkable that one of our states would go to war against another. Conflicts between, as well as within, states are settled in the courts and legislatures, not on the battlefield.

Contrast the American experience with that of Europe, which has been devastated by periodic wars throughout modern history. Now, however, thanks to the formation of the European Economic Community and a new sense of European, rather than only national, citizenship, it is difficult to imagine these former enemies going to war against each other. What happened in Philadelphia between May and September of 1787, when our federal structure was created, and what has happened in Western Europe since the Second World War, now needs to happen on a global scale to maintain lasting peace.

Every civilized country has an established system of law, courts, and limited police power to keep the peace within its society. Nearly 2000 years ago, when Paul was involved in a threatened riot in Ephesus, the town clerk declared, "If therefore Demitrius and the craftsmen have a complaint against anyone, the courts are open, and there are procounsuls; let them bring charges against one another" (Acts 19:38). They had a structure for resolving conflicts without violence. Yet the nations of the world continue to live at the stage of the legendary wild west, where the fastest gun ruled. We long ago rejected such "cow-boyism" as an uncivilized and un-Christian way of settling dis-putes within our country. Is it not long past time to reject the resolution of conflict by violence on the global scene?

There can be no lasting national security without global se-curity. Just as the development of the cannon made the fortified castle obsolete, the development of nuclear devices has made the independently secure nation-state obsolete. There is no security in a fortified compartment on a sinking ship, nor is there security within the borders of a fortified nation on a dying planet.

Therefore, humanity's challenge is to create a global security system strong enough to preserve the peace and limited enough that it cannot become a source of tyranny. I believe that we, as members of the global community in Christ, are not only called to live with planetary perspective, but also that we are to take the lead in working to create such a global security system.

If this seems a utopian dream, note that it only asks for the global application of the same kind of security system operating in every civilized nation. The institutions of feudalism gave way to the institutions of the nation-state. Now the institution of the totally sovereign and independently secure nation-state must give way to global security. When such change seems impossible, remember these words of Edvard Hambro: "Politics is the art of making possible tomorrow what seems impossible today," and this statement from Norman Cousins, "All things are possible once enough human beings realize that the whole of the human future is at stake." If we lack the imagination and courage to make this transition, human survival is in doubt. Our choice is coexistence or nonexistence, one world or no world.

A global security system does not mean the end of nations. The creation of the federal government of the United States did not abolish the states. Those states, in effect, invested a portion of their sovereignty in the federal authority and thereby found security that would have been impossible independently. When

Carl Van Doren wrote of the transition from independent and sometimes warring colonies to "united states" within a federal union, he titled his book *The Great Rehearsal*. He saw the creation of our federation of states as a model of what needs to happen on a global scene if humanity is to survive. With similar insight, Emery Reves has written in *The Anatomy of Peace* of how the nations of the world must move beyond what he calls "the new polytheism" of independent nations, each acting as its own "god," and into a new global community. From before its founding, Reves recognized that the tragic flaw in plans for the United Nations was failure to deal with the problem of unlimited national sovereignty. An adequate global security system should not be a planetary world government, but it will require authority appropriate to its responsibility.

Models for such a security system can be seen in the proposals of The World Federalists, and in writings such as *World Peace through World Law* by Clark and Sohn, which calls for specific restructuring and strengthening of the United Nations. Richard Hudson's proposal for a "binding triad" to override the veto in the United Nations when two-thirds of the world's nations, people, and wealth are in agreement, offers a simple but significant step in the right direction. Groups such as Global Education Associates and the World Citizens Movement help change our thinking toward the global perspectives necessary for the creation of global security.

Advocating proposals like *World Peace through World Law,* which calls for an international police force, may seem inconsistent with my call for the abolition of war but there are fundamental differences between peacemaking police power and war-making military power. Police power operates under the rule of law, in conjunction with courts of justice and with limited, lethal means. The purpose of a responsible police force is not to kill people but to bring criminals into courts of justice, where they are tried for their crimes. Military power, as now established, operates within an almost nonexistent structure of international law and in relation to an essentially powerless world court. There is no limit, beyond a government's ability or desire, on the lethal capacities of any nation. The purpose of war-making military power is not to bring people into courts of justice, but to bring them to their knees or to their graves. No responsible police force would measure its success by the "body count" of those killed or by the destruction of property it had devastated, but these are among the historic marks of military achievement.

Military power is not just an extension of police power; it is an aberration and distortion of police power. Responsible police power is an alternative to irresponsible military power, and can be part of a global security system created as part of a functional alternative to war. Police power differs from military power in kind as well as in degree. An international police force would be limited by international law in size, composition, and weaponry, as well as by the circumstances in which it could be used. It would operate in conjunction with international courts of justice that would have authority to enforce their decisions by political and economic means as well as by police power. It would act only as a last resort, following failure of negotiations and all other sanctions. As part of a global security system, an international police force would operate under constraints remarkably similar to those expressed in Christian just/unjust-war theories. For the first time, those theories would have a chance of being put into practice. Therefore, I believe it is consistent to call for the establishment of such a global security system while at the same time urging the abolition of the current war-making system.

Building bridges

When pioneers journeyed westward, their progress was thwarted by the Mississippi River. The immediate solution was to build ferryboats to carry travelers from one bank to the other.

Clearly, however, this was an inadequate and temporary solution. Dozens of bridges had to be built in order to unite the nation.

Relations among the nations of the world are now at the ferryboat stage. The United Nations is an extremely useful facilitator of ferryboat traffic. If it ceased to exist, we would have to recreate it tomorrow. But it is a flawed organization. The world must move beyond ferryboating to bridge building. Those bridges do not yet exist. Their construction will be difficult and dangerous. The task of creating an interlinked global security system with strength for peacemaking and safeguards against its own abuse is one of the most difficult to ever confront humanity. Risks abound: a global security system may fail to keep the peace; it may become oppressive and tyrannical. The challenge is awesome, but when tempted to turn aside, we remember the alternative—continued "cowboyism" on an international scale! The wild west with atomic six-guns! The end of civilization! No more singing birds and laughing children! No more symphony concerts and picnics in the park! A planet populated by insects less susceptible than ourselves to the sickening effects of radiation! The challenge is awesome, but it must be met. The future of humanity depends on it!

When asked why humanity continued to have so many conflicts after achieving such scientific advances, Einstein replied, "politics is more difficult than physics." The creation of a global security system is difficult, but not impossible. Here is a challenge worthy of the world's best minds and most courageous patriots. If it is to happen, some of our national leaders, from east and west and north and south, will need to act with the daring of Anwar Sadat in his journey to Jerusalem and Richard Nixon in his visit to China. We must abandon the old modes of tribal thinking which perpetuate drift toward catastrophe. We must think and act anew to create a world of global security for ourselves tomorrow and for our children and children's children for generations upon generations yet to be.

We have imagined the structure of peace as a three-sided tower built on a solid foundation. Justice is the foundation; reconciliation and global security are two of the walls. Peace through the way of the cross is the third wall necessary to complete the structure.

PEACE THROUGH THE WAY OF THE CROSS

The cross of Jesus reveals the Christlike way of confronting and ultimately triumphing over evil. Where love meets sin and keeps on loving, there is the place of the cross. We thank God for the mercy and eternal hope revealed and promised in the cross.

While confessing the cross as our hope and salvation and rightly insisting on "a theology of the cross" rather than "a theology of glory," we have often, in effect, taken the cross by the short end, sharpened the other into a sword, and gone to war for the glory of the state. Although central to our theology and personal faith, the cross has continued to be peripheral, and often incidental, to our personal and corporate way of life.

The cross of Christ witnesses not only to our redemption, but also to the cost of Christlike living in a sinful world. In Christ we are called not only to trust in the gospel of the cross but also to follow Jesus in living the way of the cross. Such Christlike living meets hatred with love and is more willing to suffer than to inflict suffering. It may even mean willingness to die rather than to kill.

In his crisis hour, as in all of his earthly pilgrimage, Jesus rejected the way of the sword and chose to live the way of the cross. He did not call legions of angels to come to his defense. Jesus told an impulsive defender, "Put your sword back into its place; for all who take the sword will perish by the sword" (Matt. 26:52). The parallel passage in Luke is even more emphatic. There Jesus says of use of the sword, "No more of this!" (Luke 22:51).

Some discount Jesus' emphatic rejection of the sword by pointing out that he also said, "I have not come to bring peace but a sword" (Matt. 10:34). But the parallel passage in Luke 12:51 makes it clear that the "sword" Jesus brings refers to "division" within families resulting from commitment to follow Christ, not to the literal sword Jesus ordered put away and not used again.

Renouncing the sword can lead to suffering. It did so for Jesus and also for his disciples, who, from a military standpoint, were left defenseless and were martyred for their faith. It is sobering to think about all of the innocent people, beginning with the children slaughtered by Herod (Matt. 2:16), who have suffered and died in the wake of the life and witness of Jesus. Jesus taught his disciples to expect to be treated as he had been treated, and he did not provide them with any lethal means of defense.

What about Hitler?

When someone urges renunciation of the sword, the usual reply is that such obedience to Jesus is unrealistic and irresponsible. Objectors will underscore the need for force in a sinful world and probably ask, "What about Hitler?" With Hitler's armies on the march, there may have been nothing else to do but to take up arms against Hitler. It certainly would have been wrong to do nothing. Passivity in the face of evil would, as Gandhi pointed out, be worse than opposition by military force. If there ever was a case for justifiable warfare, there can be little doubt that Hitler's aims and tactics provided justification for it and also, on the other hand, justification for refusing to take up arms to support it. Granting this, however, does not mean that there was nothing but military might that could have undermined Hitler's power and prevented the horrors of the Second World War and the Holocaust. It is not enough to ask whether it is justifiable to go to war against someone like Hitler. We must also ask where people like Hitler get their power.

It is a fact of political life, underscored by Etienne de la Boétre in his book *On Voluntary Serfdom* in the 16th century, and re-emphasized by Gene Sharp and others today, that *all leaders receive their power from the cooperation of their people.* Political power does not reside in anyone. Hitler did not possess that power in himself. He received it from the cooperation of his people. To be sure, he both evoked and coerced that obedience. Millions were moved by Hitler's rhetoric and millions more by fear of what would happen to them and their loved ones if they refused to cooperate. But this fact remains: Hitler's power depended on the cooperation of millions of people, from his closest cohorts on down through a chain of willing and coerced persons to the lowest-ranking draftee in his army and the most humble citizen of his society.

Given the power Hitler received from the obedience of his people, there may have been no alternative to war against him. But what if Hitler had not had that cooperation? What if half, or even one-fourth, or one-tenth, of the Christians had refused to cooperate with Hitler? What if millions had been given the courage to say, "I will die before I will fight in this unjust war or support the Holocaust"? Widespread noncooperation early in Hitler's rise to power might have persuaded many that Hitler had no future and prompted them to shift their allegiance to someone who would have succeeded Hitler in the normal political process. Had that happened, the Hitler episode might have been only a footnote in world history.

If noncooperation had begun later, after the fever of war had gripped the nation and the horrors of the "final solution" were being implemented, there would certainly have been immense suffering for those who chose civil disobedience. Martyrs might have been numbered in the millions. A cross of suffering would have been raised over Hitler's Germany the like of which the world has seldom seen. Yet, just as we can be certain of such suffering, we can also be sure that if sufficient numbers had refused to cooperate with Hitler, even to the point of death, Hitler's power would have been so undermined that he could not have carried forward either the war or the Holocaust.

Imagine that 10 million of Hitler's soldiers and civilians had been executed for total noncooperation, and that millions more had been halfhearted and careless in fulfilling their military and civilian arms-related responsibilities. Given such massive civil disobedience, Hitler's war making and Holocaust building would have ground to a halt—not only because of the persuasive effect of martyrs' courage on moral people, but because it would have diminished the tyrant's power.

The fact that leaders' political and military power comes from the cooperation of their people makes nonviolent noncooperation a potent means of combating oppressors. The history of nonviolent civil disobedience, which for people of faith is also divine obedience, demonstrates another "Jesus alternative" to violence and war. When carefully planned and persistently followed, the tactics of noncooperation, as practiced by people such as Gandhi, Martin Luther King Jr., and leaders of strikes and boycotts, have resulted in dramatic and permanent change. Strategists such as Gene Sharp, author of *The Politics of Non-Violent Action,* have spelled out its principles and tactics in concrete detail. These methods provide a functional and moral substitute for war. Pragmatically, the use of nonviolent noncooperation in what Sharp and others call "civilian-based defense" is really war with other weapons. When practiced with the motivation of the love of Christ, it is living the way of the cross.

The power of noncooperation

Opponents of nonviolent action claim that Gandhi and King were successful because they used these methods against people who were moral, if not tenderhearted, and that such tactics would never work against tyrants like Hitler. Even apart from the false and degrading assumption that the German people are inherently less moral or tenderhearted than the English and the Americans, this objection ignores a basic fact: willingness to suffer rather than to cooperate with evil not only inspires the sympathy and support of others, who often harbor similar convictions; it literally decreases a leader's power! Ten million martyrs might have stopped the war and the Holocaust. Many of the 40 to 50 million who died in Hitler's war and death camps might have lived. If 20 million had been saved at the cost of 10 million martyrs, many would still maintain that such suffering was proof that "nonviolent actions don't work." But why, after all the wars in which millions more have died, are there still so few who realize that "war doesn't work"?

Acts of nonviolent noncooperation do not always succeed. But this is also, if not more often, true of acts of violence. In war, at least one side always loses, and the results have often been disastrous for both. The success of war is especially suspect when measured in terms of correcting the problems that provoked the conflict in the first place. It is essential, as von Clausewitz emphasizes in *On War,* to distinguish between the military aim and the political purpose of war. The military aim is always victory; the political purpose is the fruit of victory. The problem in evaluating the success of war is that when the fighting begins, the political purpose is often forgotten, and the sole concern is to win. After winning, the victor holds a celebration, and declares the war a great success. Nevertheless, that war may have utterly failed to achieve its political purpose and the winner may, in fact, be far worse off at the end than at the beginning.

In this sense our war against Hitler was less than fully successful. Near the end of the war, a Nazi leader is reported to have said, "Hitler will be defeated but Hitlerism will prevail in the world." Ponder that statement. "Superpowers" have succeeded the "superman" in threatening civilization. Tyrannies sustained by military power continue to oppress their people and harrass their neighbors. All humanity now wakes, works, and sleeps under what John Kennedy called "the nuclear sword of Damocles." Too much "Hitlerism" abounds in our world. Can we, therefore, really rejoice over the "success" of even our most glorious war?

Wars plant the seeds from which new wars and new tyrannies grow. The First World War, which was fought "to end all wars" and to "keep the world safe for democracy," helped create the conditions which spawned both the Second World War and the rise of communism. War also enables horrors otherwise impossible. Can we imagine, for example, that Hitler's "final solution" could have been entertained, let alone implemented, apart from the context of total war? Therefore, we must as least question the continued validity of war and begin to consider nonviolent alternatives that do not threaten the survival of humanity.

Another need—training for nonviolence

Immense amounts of brainpower and money have been dedicated to learning and practicing war. Millions have received basic military training. War colleges and national academies prepare military leaders. One-fourth to one-third of our scientists and engineers work in arms research and development. U.S. military spending is nearly a billion dollars a day.

In contrast, the resources of mind and money devoted to learning the art of conquering oppressors by nonviolent means have been infinitesimally small. In light of the fact that those who have chosen the way of noncooperation and civil disobedience have usually acted spontaneously, with little or no training, their impact has been amazing. Imagine the power of people trained from childhood in the arts of nonviolent noncooperation and mobilized to stand together.

Pragmatic versus spiritual, nonviolent action

It is also important to distinguish between pragmatic and loving noncooperation. To illustrate, think of two people side by side on a picket line during an industrial strike. One is motivated by greed and inspired by hatred toward company management. For this striker, noncooperation is an act of coercive and even vengeful power. The use of violence has been pragmatically rejected as counterproductive. This striker's aim is not to exert a positive moral influence, but to force an agreement satisfactory to the workers.

The other striker is not motivated by greed and hatred, but by love for both the workers, who are being treated unjustly, and for the management, which is perceived to be well-meaning but misguided. This striker wants to convert, not just coerce, the management and hopes that the restraint of nonviolent action will evoke a sympathetic response from everyone involved.

In reality, the motives of most strikers are more mixed and less sharply divided than our example suggests. In international conflict the difference in motivation would likely be more marked than on the picket line. Some "warriors" using the weapons of nonviolent noncooperation might be as hateful and vindictive as those using guns and bombs. Others' nonviolent resistance might be motivated by the kind of love revealed by Gandhi, Martin Luther King Jr., and, above all, by Jesus on the cross.

Is it appropriate for those motivated by the love of Christ to stand together with the pragmatic practitioners of nonviolence who are motivated by hatred? I believe that nonviolent people with differing motivations can work together. If we insist on working only with the purely motivated, we will ultimately work with nobody, not even ourselves. John once said to Jesus, "Teacher, we saw a man casting out demons in your name, and we forbade him, because he was not following us." Jesus replied, "Do not forbid him; for no one who does a mighty work in my name will be able soon after to speak evil of me. For he that is not against us is for us" (Mark 9:38-40) Noncooperation with evil out of base motives is better than either violent resistance or passive inaction. Those who act against evil out of impure motives are not against us but for us, and when their actions are right, we do well to stand together.

As we are loved in our sins, we are commissioned in Christ to love all other sinners, including the enemies who oppress us. At the same time we are to hate the sin and to express a full measure of righteous wrath through noncooperation with every practice of injustice and every institution of oppression that degrades and destroys the lives of people. With Gandhi we see noncooperation with evil to be our sacred duty. At the same time we do not disdain the pragmatic advocates of nonviolence who challenge us with exhortations such as these from Gene Sharp: "If you don't want the fire to burn stop putting wood on it. If you don't want the plant to grow, stop watering it. If you don't want the beast to stand at your door stop feeding it."

Civilian-based defense

"Civilian-based defense" using nonviolent noncooperation doesn't always work. Like war, it is costly in pain and suffering. It is difficult to teach and more difficult to practice consistently. But there is also much to be said for it. It does not threaten the annihilation of the human species or the destruction of civilization. Even when practiced pragmatically, it is far more in harmony with the way of the cross than is the way of violence and war. Just as hateful and lustful thoughts, though sinful, are clearly preferable to murder and rape, spiteful noncooperation with evil is clearly preferable to violence and war.

When we remember that Jesus taught us to go the second mile, turn the other cheek, love our enemies, pray for those who persecute us, do good to those who abuse us, treat others as we wish to be treated, and to love others even as he loves us, we must confess that our attitudes and actions are often out of line with Jesus' teaching. When asked his opinion of the Bible, Nikita Khrushchev replied that he did not agree with Jesus' statements about loving our enemies and turning the other cheek. Khrushchev declared that if someone were to strike him on one cheek he would not turn the other but would instead "knock his block off!" As we honestly examine ourselves as individuals and as a nation, isn't it true that we are often more faithful followers of Khrushchev than of Christ?

When Roland Bainton was told during the Khrushchev era that to follow the way of Christ would mean that we would all become slaves of Khrushchev, he replied that he did not think that this was true, but that even if it were true, "I would still follow Christ!" It would be awesome to make such a decision, but let us not be naive about the alternative. "Better dead than Red" may be true for a heroic individual, but it is certainly not true for the human race. Living in Moscow or Peking today is clearly preferable to living in Hiroshima and Nagasaki on August 6 and 9, 1945.

Nonviolent "defeat" versus violent "victory"

In this age of doomsday weapons the defeat of civilian-based defense may be preferable not only to defeat, but even to "victory," in a nuclear war. How we could live following a "victory" in which our nation had been responsible for the deaths of tens of millions of innocent human beings? Gene Sharp also points out that

> . . . even failure after an heroic struggle by civilian-based defense is preferable to any outcome of a major nuclear war. At worst it would mean a long, difficult, and painful existence under severe tyranny, but life would still remain and with life the hope for eventual freedom. . . . Non-violent action is not of course for cowards. It requires the ability to sustain the battle whatever the price and suffering, yet would, in any case, allow for a future for humanity . . . in this type of struggle the failure to achieve total victory does not mean total defeat.[9]

It should also be emphasized that the military conquest of a country that is mobilized for civilian-based defense does not mean the defeat of that country or the enslavement of its people. Military defeat is almost always regarded as the end of the war, but for those who are armed with the weapons of noncooperation, military defeat may mean that the nonviolent struggle has only begun.

Even without training in the arts of nonviolent resistance, it would be utterly impossible for either the United States or the Soviet Union to occupy or control the other. The Soviet Union wouldn't dare to send millions of troops to live in all corners of the United States. They would not only fear guerrilla attacks at every outpost but also that their troops would be so captivated by the American way of life that they would return as revolutionaries or perhaps decide not to return at all. Although it seems shocking and absurd at first thought, it would be clearly preferable for both the United States and the Soviet Union to freely open their borders for occupation by the other than to annihilate each other in nuclear war. When "armed" with carefully prepared civilian-based defense, such an action would not be to surrender to each other but to continue the battle with more rational weapons. In such a non-military contest the balance of power would be overwhelmingly on the side of the United States. The chances of freedom, democracy, and free enterprise surviving such nonviolent conflict are far greater than the likelihood of their rising to bloom again from the ashes of a nuclear holocaust.

Something in us seems to prefer the macho triumphs of the sword to the quiet victories won through the way of the cross. We prefer to die fighting rather than to die loving. Yet the cross stands as witness to another way. Christ calls us to love rather than to hate, to suffer rather than to inflict suffering, to die rather than to kill, to live the way of the cross rather than the way of the sword. Then we are to teach that way to our children and to the citizenry at large. As we live the way of the cross, Christ also promises to be with us in the fullness of God's love and power, to sustain and bless us, and to make our lives a blessing to others.

Is civil disobedience Christian?

Having advocated nonviolent, civilian-based defense as a functional alternative to war, I must now add a more specific response to those who are certain to object to the use of civil disobedience by Christians. They are quick to quote, "Let every person be subject to the governing authorities. For there is no authority except from God and those that exist have been instituted by God. Therefore he who resists the authorities resists what God has appointed, and those who resist will incur judgment" (Rom. 13:1-2). It is essential that we see this statement in context. The preceding paragraph develops the theme, "Bless those who persecute you; bless and do not curse them" (Rom. 12:14). The verses that follow declare, "For rulers are not a terror to good conduct, but to bad. Would you have no fear of him who is in authority? Then do what is good, and you will receive his approval, for he is God's servant for your good" (Rom. 13:3-4). In the same passage Paul goes on to state that we are to "be subject, not only to avoid God's wrath but also for the sake of conscience" (Rom. 13:5) and that we are to "owe no one anything, except to love one another" (Rom. 13:8). "Love," says Paul, "does no wrong to a neighbor; therefore love is the fulfilling of the law" (Rom. 13:10).

It is clear from even such a quick survey of this passage that it does not advocate total obedience to rulers who are a "terror to good conduct," who can't be obeyed "for the sake of conscience, and who command us to "do wrong to our neighbor." How can we obey commands to harm someone when we are to "owe no one anything, except to love one another" (Rom. 13:8)? To interpret Romans 13 without these reservations is to accuse the apostle Paul of commanding idolatrous submission to the state, which, like all other idolatries, would be utterly abhorrent to both his ancient Jewish tradition and his new Christian convictions.

Opponents of the Christian use of civil disobedience often quote the words of Jesus, "Render to Caesar the things that are Caesar's, and to God the things that are God's" (Mark 12:17), but do not always distinguish between what belongs to God and what belongs to Caesar. From everything we know about Jesus, it is clear that he understood that our conscience, supreme loyalty, and indeed very life, do not belong to Caesar, but to God. Therefore, for a Christian to tell the government, "I will always obey no matter what you ask of me," is not patriotism but idolatry.

Colin Morris suggests another interesting interpretation of this passage. In response to the question, "Is it right to pay tribute to Caesar or not? Should we pay or should we not?" Morris replies:

> One has only to ask: What, in the eyes of the devout Jew, legitimately belonged to Caesar in the Holy Land? The answer is—nothing. The Romans had invaded the land of a free people, they ruled by no other sanction than force, and extracted tribute as a form of brigandage. Throughout their long history, the Jews had never wavered in their belief that everything that touched them, their land, its people, and its wealth, belonged to God. If God had his due, Caesar would get nothing . . . . It is as though members of the Underground in Occupied Europe had asked a patriot whose judgment they respected whether they ought to help the Nazis ransack their country of its treasures and had received the reply, "Give the Nazis what is coming to them!"

Such a reply in that context would have been a clear rejection of subservience to Hitler. Morris understands Jesus' reply to be a similar rejection of obedience to Caesar. He then goes on to point out that:

> The people were obviously satisfied with [Jesus'] answer: They gave a rousing welcome as he entered Jerusalem, and openly talked of him as Messiah. They may have misunderstood the nature of Jesus' mission, but never for a second would they have countenanced a collaborator with Rome as God's chosen leader. Therefore, they must have interpreted the answer of Jesus to the Pharisees and Herodians as a resounding "No!"[10]

In defense of this interpretation we note that Jesus was later accused of "perverting our nation, and forbidding us to give tribute to Caesar" (Luke 23:2).

If Morris is correct, it does not follow that Christians should never pay taxes. We are to give our government what it has coming in order to provide for the common good of all its citizens. But that does not mean that Christians are morally obligated to give their lives or their money to support every tyrant or every unjustifiable war. As we respect the right of Christian pacifists to conscientiously object to participation in all warfare, and the right of Christians within the just/unjust-war tradition to refuse to participate in wars they believe to be unjustifiable, we should also respect the right of Christians to take a similar stand of conscientious objection against the payment of taxes for purposes they believe to be morally abhorrent.

"Our money," as Harry Emerson Fosdick liked to say, "is our time and talent in portable form." Therefore, it is highly inconsistent for a conscientious objector to refuse to participate in warfare or war making while at the same time, in effect, paying someone else to do so. In an attempt to overcome this inconsistency, many Christians have joined in support of proposals in Congress for the establishment of a "U.S. Peace Tax Fund," which would provide a channel into peacemaking projects for the money of those who conscientiously object to its use in war making.

In the absence of such legislation, some Christians have chosen to act in civil disobedience by refusing to pay the portion of their taxes that would go to military purposes. Others have withheld the smaller percentage that would be used for the development and maintenance of doomsday weapons, and still others have chosen to withhold only a small, token amount as a symbol of the sincerity of their objection to unjustifiable military spending. Whatever our specific response to such actions, every serious Christian must wrestle with the question, Can I pray for peace while I continue to pay for war? Organizations like Conscience and the Military Tax Campaign can help to provide information and examples to motivate our thinking in this regard.

Divine obedience

Divine obedience resulting in civil disobedience has a long and noble history. In the book of Exodus we read that "the midwives feared God, and did not do as the king of Egypt commanded them, but let the male children live." When the king complained, they lied to deceive him. God blessed this disobedience and deception and "dealt well with the midwives" (See Exod. 1:15-21). The story then tells of similar disobedience to Pharaoh's order that "every son that is born to the Hebrews you shall cast into the Nile" (Exod. 1:22). This noncooperation saved the life of Moses who was to lead the people out of their bondage in Egypt (see Exod. 2:1-10).

1 Samuel 22:11-17 tells how King Saul's guards refused to obey his order to kill the priests of the Lord and how they became martyrs for their faith. The story of Esther, who was challenged to risk her life on behalf of the Jews, reports that she declared, "I will go to the King, though it is against the law; and if I perish, I perish" (Esther 4:16).

The New Testament perspective concerning divine obedience is most clearly stated in the witness of Peter and the Apostles: "We must obey God rather than men" (Acts 5:29). While urging regular obedience to civil authority, the *Augsburg Confession* also states that "when commands of civil authority cannot be obeyed without sin, we must obey God rather than men (Acts 5:29)" (Article 16). These statements from the book of Acts and the *Augsburg Confession* express the core conviction of "Human Law and the Conscience of Believers," adopted by the 1984 convention of the American Lutheran Church. I commend this statement to you as a conservative, biblical affirmation of Christian civil disobedience resulting from divine obedience.

Tests of justifiable civil disobedience

Centuries ago, Christian thinkers developed lists of criteria for justifiable warfare. I believe that the Christian church in our time should develop similar tests concerning justifiable, nonviolent noncooperation and civil disobedience. It is important to note, for example, that these methods, like military weapons, can be used for unjustifiable purposes, with impure motives and in ways that are ultimately destructive of the good of society. Christian criteria for justifiable, nonviolent action should include considerations such as the following.

A. Nonviolent noncooperation is required:
   1. when we are commanded to act contrary to the will of God; then, we obey God rather than human authority.
   2. before resorting to violence; all appropriate means of nonviolent noncooperation must be utilized prior to resorting to violence.
B. Nonviolent noncooperation is justifiable;
   1. only after negotiation and persuasion have failed.
   2. when the cause is just—to correct injustice and oppression—and never for greed, vengeance or retaliation.
   3. when the means are appropriate and proportionate to the ends, and not when resulting in more harm than good. Unwise nonviolent action can be counterproductive.
   4. when affirmative of the basic structure of society. Those who break the law must be willing to endure the penalties of disobedience.
   5. when affirmative of the pro-life principle—to preserve and enhance life but not to take it.

Although justifiable warfare requires a reasonable prospect of success, this is not always necessary for nonviolent action. Many have followed Christ in the way of divine obedience even when it meant more suffering than success. Their faithfulness has been a witness and challenge to us all.

Christians considering civil disobedience should do so in the context of prayer for guidance of the Holy Spirit, study of Scripture, and consultation with committed Christians. It is usually best to act as a group, but there are times when conscience compels acting alone and against the advice of faithful but fearful friends. They may need to be told, as Jesus told Peter, "Get behind me, Satan! You are a hindrance to me; for you are not on the side of God, but of men" (Matt. 16:23).

Beware of idolatry

Without continued vigilance, we are in danger of drifting into a subtle, but serious and sinful form of idolatry that is illustrated by two examples from the Old Testament. Aaron not only encouraged worship of the golden calf, he also proclaimed that "Tomorrow shall be a feast to the Lord" (Exod. 32:5). One day they worshiped an idol and the next the true God. Similarly, 2 Kings tells of those who "feared the Lord but also served their own gods" (2 Kings 17:33). The sin of these people was not atheism but polytheism. They trusted false gods in addition to the true God.

Likewise, even while sincerely confessing Jesus Christ and worshiping the one true God, we too are tempted to trust and worship the false gods of material wealth, national prestige, military power, and technological wizardry. Most of our idols are not bad things, but good things elevated by our trust and adoration to the place of God. Money, national security, and technology are all good, but none is God. Our problem is not always that we have no God, but often that we have too many gods—not that we are atheists, but that we are polytheists. We should never forget that "You shall have no other gods before me" (Exod. 20:3; Deut. 5:7) can also be translated "You shall have no other gods besides me." The biblical witness is clear—we are to have no other gods before or beside the one true God. We are to have no other god, period!

Although the Old Testament frequently describes the Lord as a "jealous God" (see Exod. 20:5; 34:14; Deut. 4:24; 6:15), our false gods are not jealous. They are glad to be worshiped beside or even beneath the one true God. They do not demand our total allegiance, but only our daily obedience. The god of the state, for example, does not always insist that we abandon prayer and worship, but only that we submit to its authority and obey its commands. It is especially pleased when our religious faith serves to sustain our idolatrous patriotism.

To be accused of idolatry, and even of polytheism, may seem incomprehensible and preposterous. We may protest, saying, "I don't worship material things; I thank God for them. I don't worship the state; I believe in one nation under God. I don't worship military might; I believe it defends freedom, democracy, and even Christianity itself. I don't make a god of science and technology; these are God's gifts for our good." With such thinking we seek to maintain a comfortable accommodation between our culture and our Christian faith. But the question remains— are we in fact idolatrous polytheists who trust, serve, and worship many false gods, while at the same time continuing to confess that Jesus is Lord?

When we are called at last to give account of our lives and the truth is fully revealed, we may be surprised to discover that our greatest sins were not in those things of which we were most ashamed but in those of which we were most proud—our wealth, our being number one as persons and as a nation, our power to intimidate, dominate, and destroy. Having wealth and power, we easily adopt a fortress mentality and become committed above all else to protecting what is ours. Captured by our culture and worshiping its false gods, we forget that we are called in Christ to love and to be vulnerable. Trusting in "saviors" of human creation, we abandon the security of God's grace and even become willing to sacrifice ourselves and our children on the altars of these false gods.

Repent and live

It is easy for us to see that our enemies are materialistic militarists, and that they trust and worship false gods of their own devising. It is not so easy for us to see and confess our own idolatries. Can it be that in the sight of God we are much alike? The form of our sins may be different but, in substance they are the same. If we are alike in our sins, then we are also alike in being called to repent, to turn from our sin and folly, and to act in ways appropriate to our repentance. Central to such repentance is willingness to act with divine obedience, even when that means to stand against human authority and to follow Christ in living the way of the cross.

In 1957, General of the Army Omar N. Bradley declared:

> We are now speeding inexorably towards a day when even the ingenuity of our scientists may be unable to save us from the consequences of a single rash act or a lone reckless hand on the switch of an uninterceptable missile.
>
> . . . This irony can probably be compounded a few more years, or perhaps even a few decades. Missiles will bring anti-missiles and anti-missiles will bring anti-anti-missiles. But inevitably, this whole electronic house of cards will reach a point where it can be constructed no higher. . . . When that time comes there will be little we can do other than to settle down uneasily, smother our fears, and attempt to live in a thickening shadow of death.

Then Bradley went on to ask:

> Have we already gone too far . . .? Is there any way to halt this trend—or must we push on with new devices until we inevitably come to judgment before the atom?

In response to his own question, General Bradley replied:

> I believe there is a way out . . . [But] until we get started, we shall never know what can be done.[11]

I too "believe there is a way out." In Jesus there are alternatives to the way and violence and war. There is still time to start thinking and living the Jesus way. The witness of Christ and the urgency of the present crisis join in calling us to repent and live.

In an earlier crisis, Martin Luther King Jr. spoke to a specific aspect of the repentance we need: "We will have to repent in this generation not merely for the hateful words and actions of bad people, but for the appalling silence of the good people."[12] To stand silent while evil triumphs—to fail to act when we know how to avert disaster—these are horrendous sins. To repent and to act is our opportunity and our obligation in Christ.

Harry Emerson Fosdick provided a model for our repentance. During the First World War he preached blessings on war to our soldiers in Europe. In "penitant reparation" he later confessed:

> The encouragement I gave to war is a deep self-condemnation in my heart. . . . Is there anything more infernal than this, to take the best that is in man and use it to do what war does? This is the ultimate description of war—it is the prostitution of the noblest powers of the human soul to the most dastardly deeds, the most abysmal cruelties of which our human nature is capable. That *is* war.

Thinking of how he might have preached to the Unknown Soldier, Fosdick went on:

> They sent men like me into the camps to awaken his idealism, to touch those secret holy springs within him so that with devotion, fidelity, loyalty, and self-sacrifice he might go out to war. O war, I hate you most of all for this, that you lay your hand on the noblest elements in human character, with which we might make a heaven on earth, and you use them to make a hell on earth instead. You take even our science, the fruit of our dedicated intelligence, by means of which we might here build the City of God and, using it, you fill the earth instead with new ways of slaughtering men. You take our loyalty, our unselfishness, with which we might make the earth beautiful and, using these our finest qualities, you make death fall from the sky and burst up from the sea . . . .
>
> My friends, I am not trying to make you sentimental about this. I want you to be hard-headed. We can have this monstrous thing or we can have Christ, but we cannot have both . . . .

At any rate, I will do my best to settle my account with the Unknown Soldier. I renounce war. I renounce war because of what it does to our own men. . . . I have seen the long, long hospital trains filled with their mutilated bodies. I have heard the cries of the crazed and the prayers of those who wanted to die and could not, and I remember the maimed and ruined men for whom the war is not yet over. I renounce war for what it compels us to do to our enemies, bombing their mothers . . . starving their children . . . laughing over our coffee cups about every damnable thing we have been able to do to them. I renounce war for its consequences, for the lies it lives on and propagates, for the undying hatreds it arouses, for the dictatorships it puts in the place of democracy, for the starvation that stalks after it. I renounce war and never again, directly or indirectly, will I sanction or support another! O Unknown Soldier, in penitent reparation I make you that pledge.[13]

With similar repentance we remember that:

God is our refuge and strength,
a very present help in trouble . . . .
He makes wars cease to the end of the earth;
he breaks the bow, and shatters the spear,
he burns the chariots with fire! (Ps. 46:1, 9).

Trusting in this great God, we take our stand against the institution of war and for the institutions of peace. We call and work for the abolition of the old war system and for the creation of a new peace system. As subjects of the Prince of Peace, we commit ourselves to the construction of a strong and lasting structure of peace consisting of (1) peace through justice, (2) peace through reconciliation, (3) peace through global security, and (4) peace through the way of the cross.

6 MERCY KILLING AND ITS PRO-LIFE ALTERNATIVES

      The story is told of a mother who had recently given birth to premature twins whose survival depended on the life-support system of the hospital's neonatal unit. One child, though tiny, was normal; the other was blind and severely deformed. As the mother looked at the normal child, she thanked God for the medical technology that enabled hope for a full and meaningful life, but as she looked at the deformed child who seemed destined for a world of darkness and suffering, she silently cursed the same technology that sustained its life.

That story illustrates both the joy and the anguish that accompany the life-saving developments of medical science. Doctors, families, and patients themselves now face many choices that were not available to previous generations. The use of "artificial" life-support systems inevitably leads to situations that require choices concerning the rightness or wrongness of "pulling the plug" and raises as never before the issue of mercy killing or *euthanasia*, which literally means "good death."

These changes, however, did not create the problem with which we wrestle in this chapter. The possibility of deliberately ending the life of a suffering person has always been present. We note that in at least two ways medical advances make consideration of mercy killing less pressing than in times past. One is that many formerly devastating illnesses and conditions of distressing disability can now be cured, corrected, or managed so that meaningful life is now possible. The other is that painkilling drugs eliminate much of the intense suffering formerly experienced by millions. The prospect of such suffering moved Mahatma Gandhi, who lived with great reverence for life and opposition to violence, to contemplate the possibility of being required by love and sacred duty to take the life of his own child as the only means of relieving the anguish of incurable rabies. We thank God that the comforts of modern medicine now offer alternatives for the relief of such suffering.

On the other hand, the ability to maintain biological functions that would have otherwise ceased has brought the question of euthanasia into sharper focus. The difficult cases are not those in which brain death has already occurred. When the brain is dead, the person has died. There is, therefore, no justification for maintaining the biological functions, except temporarily in order to preserve organs for transplant. The agonizing cases are those in which the person remains alive but with little, if any, prospect of healing and meaningful life.

The pro-life perspective of this book—which grants that there are tragic exceptional circumstances when the taking of life is justifiable, but which opposes all forms of institutionalized and established killing—also applies to mercy killing. That is, passive or even active euthanasia may sometimes be justifiable in a specific situation, but it is wrong when institutionalized in accepted practice, as, for example, under Hitler in the Nazi era.

Passive euthanasia

There appears to be widespread and often justifiable acceptance of passive euthanasia in the last stages of terminal illness. Few would insist on using every possible life-sustaining device to lengthen the days of every terminally ill cancer patient. Reverence for life does not necessitate the use of inhumane, "heroic" measures that prolong suffering without meaning. Responsible decisions are made regularly to refrain from the use of respirators and feeding tubes and to permit patients to die without these life supports.

The more difficult choices—emotionally, if not logically and morally—occur when these devices are already in place and the decision involves whether or not to continue their use. The consequence of the shutting off of the machines, while more dramatic, is no different in its effect from that of having decided not to use them at all. Since turning off the machine does not in itself kill the patient, this is a form of passive, or permissive, euthanasia. It allows the patient to die or to live. Karen Quinlan, for example, surprised millions by living for years after her respirator was disconnected.

Granting that passive euthanasia is sometimes justifiable does not mean that it is always so. The failure to use available medical means of sustaining life in crisis of illness or accident from which the patient could substantially recover is clearly unjustifiable. The acceptance of passive euthanasia as a personal right or established practice is emphatically to be rejected.

Criteria for justifiable, passive euthanasia

When is passive euthanasia justifiable? The basic consideration must be the welfare, and not just the immediate wish, of the patient. If the treatment, including life-support systems, offers hope of restoration to, or maintenance of, meaningful life, it should be used. If it only sustains a vegetative state or prolongs meaningless suffering, it is not required and may be compassionately rejected.

The greatest difficulties for decision making are those in which the prognosis is uncertain and the quality of future life is impossible to determine. In such cases doctors understandably, but sometimes unfairly, defer to the decision of patient and family. This is understandable, because the doctor recognizes that the outcome of a considered treatment is unknown. It can be unfair, because the patient and family are even less aware of the effects of treatment and because they are caught up in the emotional storm of the illness. It is, therefore, not surprising to hear family members ask their doctor, "What would you do if she were your mother?" This question is appropriate. It places the responsibility for prognosis and treatment where it belongs—with the medical experts and not just with the suffering patient and anguishing family. When the doctor's reply to such a question is debatable, it is also proper to seek a second or third opinion, and, when consensus is lacking, to err, if need be, on the side of life—that is, to maintain treatment.

Although realism dictates reserve in its application, another factor to be considered is that tomorrow's newspapers may carry headlines announcing a cure for the condition from which the patient is suffering. Such a dramatic development is unlikely, but possible. Even the strongest advocates of capital punishment would grant that it would be a tragic mistake to execute a criminal and then receive evidence that the person was innocent. It would be equally tragic to permit a patient to die and then discover that a cure is now available. Here, too, the medical professionals, who are most familiar with research developments, can provide the wisest counsel.

Respect for the patient's wishes?

When mentally alert, the patient should have significant, but not total, reponsibility for deciding the procedures to be followed. In most cases the fully informed patient should have the authority to receive or refuse treatment, but there are times when doctor and family should override the patient's desires. It is legitimate to limit the patient's authority when the desire to die rather than to receive treatment is in itself a symptom of a disease that can be cured or is the result of intense but temporary suffering that can be relieved. In such cases the doctor and family are justified in pursuing a course of treatment to which the patient now objects but for which they believe he or she will later be grateful.

To give a depressed and emotionally disturbed patient ultimate authority over the course of treatment abdicates medical and family responsibility. This is in effect to enable the unjustifiable suicide of the patient. Someone who is miserably seasick and asks to be thrown overboard should certainly not be granted this request. Anyone who assisted in casting such a person into the sea would be at best utterly irresponsible, and at worst a cold-blooded murderer. We all know that when such a person is once again on dry land, the nausea will disappear and gratitude for life will return. Similarly, there can be no justification for cooperating with the death wish of a pathologically suicidal or temporarily suffering person. Only when there is virtually no prospect for future gratitude and life fulfillment should a patient be permitted to die without the medical treatment that could prolong life.

Active euthanasia

Although passive euthanasia is widely accepted, there are strong emotional and legal barriers to active euthanasia. Doctors are permitted to refrain from treatments that would prolong their patients' lives, but are not allowed to administer drugs to kill them. Is such a distinction between passive and active euthanasia always morally justifiable? Are there circumstances in which it is right to practice active euthanasia?

Although it is tempting to take an absolute stand against active euthanasia, the recognition of tragic, exceptional circumstances makes it impossible for me to do so. Just as there are situations in which it may be justifiable to kill the unborn, the enemy warrior, or the criminal intent on murder, there may be also circumstances in which active euthanasia is more compassionate than passive. Is it, for example, more kind to cause death by dehydration and starvation than it is to kill the patient by lethal injection? In both cases the motive and effect are exactly the same; only the method is different. Is it possible that in some cases the sin of omission (permitting death by dehydration and starvation) may be greater than the sin of commission (causing death by lethal injection)?

Emotionally it is obviously much easier for the family and doctor to permit the patient to die than to deliberately kill the patient. But is there a similar logical and moral difference? Raising such a question reminds us of the extent to which emotion, rather than logical or moral considerations, often prevails in life and death decisions. Many people, for example, are appalled at the thought of deliberately killing their 95-year-old grandmother who has been in a coma for months and for whom there is no prospect of meaningful life; but at the same time they are advocates of abortion on demand. Is it not, however, more moral to deliberately act to end life's final suffering than to foreclose the possibility of life fulfillment at its beginning? The point of this observation is not to affirm active euthanasia (to me it is more of an argument against easy abortion), but to underscore the emotional rather than ethical basis of many of our decisions.

Risking the slippery slope?

While granting that it may be morally justifiable in exceptional circumstances, I see great danger in the cultural and legal acceptance of active euthanasia. Taking this step places our feet on a slippery slope on which we can quickly slide into easy and irreverent mercy killing for unjustifiable reasons and then on into the institutionalized and established practice of euthanasia for economic and social purposes, as practiced by Hitler. If laws are changed to permit active euthanasia in rare, justifiable circumstances, it will require extreme vigilance to prevent these exceptions from becoming standard practice.

It is reported that the average age of nursing-home residents is now 83 and rising. Medical costs continue to escalate, in spite of efforts to contain them. Some speak of the responsibility of the elderly to die in order to ease the burden on the younger generation. These signs of our times tell of increasing pressure for public acceptance of active as well as passive euthanasia. They are small steps down a road that could lead to provisions for the permitted, and possibly even required, elimination not only of the suffering, senile, and elderly, but also of others of all ages who have been determined to be nonproductive members of society. Therefore, even though there may be exceptional circumstances in which active euthanasia is justified, I believe that it is wiser public policy to continue to prohibit it altogether rather than risk the temptations and tendencies of this slippery slope.

In summary, passive euthanasia may be justifiable (1) when it is determined that the patient is irreversibly comatose, (2) when the treatment prolongs imminent and inevitable death, and (3) when the treatment itself is so traumatic that it is inhumane to administer it. In addition to these criteria, active euthanasia should never be permitted or even considered unless it is clearly inhumane to let an illness run its course and there is no other means of ending meaningless suffering.

No less care and medical assistance should be provided for the newborn than for the elderly. In fact, since all of life is still before them, they merit even more help than those at the end of life. Therefore, babies should never be allowed to die when treatment, including corrective surgery, offers hope of meaningful life.

The pro-life alternatives

The pro-life alternatives to euthanasia include everything possible to provide compassionate and often costly care of the ill, infirm, and elderly. The true test of a society's faithfulness to the pro-life perspective is not only in its opposition to killing but also in its willingness to make adequate provision for those who are suffering and nonproductive. As costs of care increase, individuals in specific circumstances and society as a whole will be strongly tempted to sell out both compassion and responsible reverence for life in exchange for economic considerations. If the day comes when euthanasia is established as an economic policy, we will have ceased to be either fully moral or fully human. It is imperative that we oppose every step toward irresponsible euthanasia and also affirm the reordering of the priorities and expenditures of our personal and corporate life in order to provide the compassionate care every human being deserves. If we are not vigilant in opposition to unjustifiable euthanasia, we may one day be haunted by horrors more antiseptic, but no less terrifying, than Hitler's "final solution."

Centuries ago, when theologians developed theories stating occasions in which Christians could justifiably participate in warfare, they could not have imagined the practical transformation of those theories into the present militarization of the planet with doomsday weapons that now threaten human survival. The first Christians to grant that abortion is justifiable in certain circumstances would also be shocked by the millions of abortions performed in the world today and by the casual acceptance of this practice by many Christians. Likewise, those of us who are willing to grant the justifiability of passive, and even active, euthanasia in some exceptional circumstances must emphatically oppose it in all others. We must maintain a consistently pro-life stance against all the establishments of death and for all that enables and enhances life. As Christians captured and controlled by the ethic of reverence for life, we should not be driven by legalistic absolutes into irreverent and irresponsible preservation of life, nor should we be compelled by callous indifference and greed into the irreverant and irresponsible taking of life. In all circumstances we seek to remain essentially and consistently pro-life people.

7 THE DEATH PENALTY AND ITS PRO-LIFE ALTERNATIVES

It is not difficult for me to imagine tragic, exceptional circumstances in which the taking of life may be justifiable. A case can be made for justifiable abortion, war, and euthanasia, but I must confess that it is not easy for me to think of situations in which it is justifiable to kill a person who has been restrained from harming others. There may be bizarre circumstances in which there is no alternative to killing a person who is already disarmed and under our control, but these are not typical death-row cases.

Christian convictions regarding capital punishment are rightly based on both biblical and pragmatic, humanitarian grounds. We will consider each in turn.

Biblical considerations

As a Christian who believes that Jesus is Lord of Scripture, I am convinced that Christ-centered biblical interpretation requires opposition to the execution of criminals. Jesus' rejection of the death penalty is recorded in the account of his confrontation with the would-be executioners of the woman caught in the act of adultery. Recalling Old Testament texts like Lev. 20:10 and Deut. 22:22, they told Jesus, "Now in the law Moses commanded us to stone such" (John 8:5). They were convinced that Scripture was on their side, but they knew enough about Jesus to wonder if he would agree with them. John tells us that when they went on to ask, "What do you say about her?" their purpose was "to test him, that they might have some charge to bring against him" (John 8:6). Jesus' response was with words so clear and striking that the woman's accusers "went away, one by one, beginning with the eldest" until "Jesus was left alone with the woman standing before him" (John 8:9).

"Let him who is without sin among you" Jesus had said, "be the first to throw a stone at her" (John 8:7). Those intending execution stood in the tradition of the Old Testament and could quote Scripture not only to permit, but to command, the death penalty, but they had no reply to the convicting and correcting word of Jesus. The eldest and wisest were the first to take it in and take their leave. They were convicted of their own sins and accepted the fact that there is no justification for the vengeful execution of one sinner by another. If all Christians had followed their example, there would have been no blessing of capital punishment in Christian history. Nor would there be many executions among us if only those without sin were to declare the sentence or throw the switch.

It is significant that the woman's accusers knew enough about Jesus to expect that he might oppose her execution. We too are not surprised by Jesus' response. We are struck by the simple profundity of his answer but are not surprised by it. We would be shocked if Jesus had said, "You are right and righteous. Go ahead and kill this wretched sinner." That would have been out of harmony with everything else we know about Jesus. Even from the cross, when Jesus himself was being executed, he prayed,

"Father, forgive them; for they know not what they do" (Luke 23:34). How then can we who are privileged to know Jesus support a practice that he specifically opposed and which is contrary to all else we know about him?

The command and example of Jesus in this text stand in clear opposition to all the commands and examples in the Old Testament that can be quoted in support of capital punishment. Several times in the New Testament Jesus is recorded as saying, "You have heard that it was said," and then he went on to refer to a specific Old Testament or rabbinic teaching which he rejected or reinterpreted by saying, "But I say to you" (see Matt. 5:38-39, etc.). In the story of the woman taken in adultery, Jesus said, in effect, "You have rightly read that the Old Testament teaches and illustrates the practice of capital punishment, but I say to you, practice it no more. Remember that you too are a sinner and that you have no right to condemn and kill another sinner who now stands helpless before you." Therefore, unless we Christians are prepared to say that this text is not an authentic witness to the teaching of Jesus, or that Jesus was wrong, or that Jesus does not reveal God's will for our lives, or that there are some among us who are not sinful, are we not compelled by Christ to oppose capital punishment?

Prior to his conversion, the apostle Paul was present at the stoning of Stephen, and is described as "consenting to his death" (Acts 8:1). As a new person in Christ, Paul repented of his vengeful attitudes and actions and must have had his own sins in mind when he wrote, "Beloved, never avenge yourselves, but leave it to the wrath of God; for it is written 'Vengeance is mine, I will repay, says the Lord' " (Rom. 12:19). When heinous crimes are committed, it is understandable that many call for vengeance. When wronged, we are all tempted to retaliate and to avenge ourselves. But as we know Jesus, we also understand that such is not the spirit of Christ. We are rightly appalled at the practice of ancient societies that sacrificed human beings to appease their gods. Should not we followers of Jesus be equally appalled by the legalized sacrifice of human beings to appease the gods of the state and vengeful public opinion through the practice of capital punishment? When "the love of Christ controls us" (2 Cor. 5:14), hatred and vengeance are driven out, and replaced by compassion and forgiveness.

Pragmatic, humanitarian considerations

In addition to the witness of Jesus there are also pragmatic, humanitarian grounds for rejecting the death penalty.

Many advocates of capital punishment believe that executing criminals deters crime. There is, however, little, if any, evidence that this is true. If the death penalty had a significant deterrent effect on would-be murderers, there would be much less murder in societies that practice capital punishment than in those that do not, but, in fact, homicide rates are frequently higher in countries and states that practice capital punishment. Some may even kill in order to arrange for their own "suicides" by dramatic execution.

Instead of deterring murder and other crime, the violence of capital punishment may actually serve to stimulate the spirit of violence within a society. By maintaining that killing is an acceptable form of coercion and retaliation, the government sets an example for all who are frustrated by those who stand in the way of their perverse desires. When the state tells its citizens, "Behave or we will kill you," it is, in effect, inviting its people to say the same to one another.

If evidence could be produced to demonstrate some deterrent effect, this in itself would not be sufficient justification for the practice of capital punishment. We might deter petty thievery by cutting off the hands of thieves, but we do not do so because we recognize that such behavior is barbaric and inhumane. Yet is not the literal or figurative decapitation of a criminal a far greater barbarism than cutting off the hand of a thief? If the lesser bar-barism is morally repugnant to us, by what logic, or emotion, do we advocate the greater?

Some support capital punishment on the grounds that it dem-onstrates reverence for life over against those who cheapen life by committing murder. But how does taking life increase respect for life? Killing murderers in order to enhance reverence for life is similar to raping rapists in order to increase respect for the sanctity of sex. Such practice would certainly have the opposite effect. Similarly, taking life only diminishes reverence for life. Killing people is no way to teach that it is wrong to kill people!

Capital punishment should also be rejected because, in practice, it discriminates not only against the poor and minorities—who cannot afford the legal counsel that enables most of the rich to avoid execution—but also because it discriminates against men. It is reported that while 40% of all homicides are committed by women, only 1% of death-row inmates are women and that only 32 of the 3,863 executions since 1930 were of women. Imagine that those numbers were reversed and that 3,831 women and only 32 men had been executed since 1930. Would America's women, liberated or not, tolerate such discrimination against themselves? Why then do men, and sensitive women, tolerate such discrim-ination against men?

Capital punishment is also based on the unwarranted assump-tion that the innocent are never convicted and that later evidence cannot shed new light on a criminal case. It is tragic when an innocent person spends years in prison only to be released fol-lowing someone else's confession or through discovery of new evidence establishing innocence. It is certainly a far greater crime, and sin, to execute an innocent person. Those who practice capital punishment play at being God, who alone is all-knowing and who alone has ultimate authority over life and death.

It may sometimes be necessary to take the life of a dangerous person in order to protect the lives of others, but this is not the case when the alternative of safe—and, if necessary, permanent—imprisonment is available. Some will argue that such incarceration is too expensive and that it is cheaper for a society to execute criminals. It is true that lethal injection costs less than a lifetime of food and shelter, but the cost of litigation in capital punishment cases is often so much greater than those in which the death penalty is not involved that some executions cost more than lifetime imprisonment. But even if execution were always cheaper than incarceration, is that really a valid reason for practicing capital punishment? How can anyone claim to be pro-life and put such a price tag on the life of another human being?

Consideration of the many factors that contribute to violence and murder within society raises issues larger than can be discussed in detail in this brief chapter. Visits with prison chaplains have convinced me that reform of our penal system is an urgent challenge of high priority. Too many of our prisons are graduate schools for instruction and inspiration in criminality. A spirit of vengeance instead of wisdom and compassion seems often to prevail. We have much to learn from the experience of those states and countries that have been most successful in controlling and rehabilitating persons prone to violence.

A society that tolerates, and even glorifies, celebration with alcohol and drugs should, at least, exercise some compassion toward those who are frequently driven by addiction to commit acts of violence. Communities that affirm the right of every citizen to own a gun should, at least, have mercy on those who prove incapable of its responsible use. But for Christians those "at leasts" are not enough. We should redouble our efforts to eliminate every form of unhealthy dependence on chemicals. I do not advocate return to prohibition, but believe that we should not permit the advertising that promises joy and peace through the use of alcohol and drugs. Without alienating all the hunters in America, do we really need to tolerate the traffic in handguns and other nonsporting weapons that helps to contribute to many more deaths of family and friends by accident or spiteful impulse than to lives saved by use of guns in self-defense?

We should also ponder the fact that the death penalty has been abolished in all of Western Europe, Canada, and Mexico, and that it is most frequently practiced in Iran, South Africa, and the Soviet Union. Are these the kinds of societies on which we should model our behavior? Amnesty International "identifies imposition of the death penalty as a violation of fundamental human rights and works for its abolition worldwide." A. I. also states that "The United States is the only Western industrial democracy which still practices capital punishment" and that they have made the "abolition of the death penalty [in the United States] a priority for the organization."

A recent church publication described capital punishment as "an issue over which Christians can reasonably disagree." In past centuries church leaders issued discussion papers concerning slavery in which they made similar statements. Many Christians in South Africa claim similar freedom to "reasonably disagree" concerning apartheid. I hope that no Christians or humanitarians among us still believe that slavery and apartheid are issues over which we can "reasonably disagree." It is also my fervent hope and prayer that the Christians and humanitarians of the world will unite as consistent, pro-life people to hasten the day when capital punishment and all other institutions of death will no longer be accepted among us.

8 WHAT ONE PERSON CAN DO

When pro-life people confronting unjustifiable abortion, war, euthanasia, capital punishment, and other evils are tempted to ask, "What can one person do?" they should remember someone's claim that "every revolution in human history began as a one-person revolution." One person had a new thought and dared to act in a new way. From that center, like the ripples on a pond from the impact of a single pebble, influence for change spread out in all directions. None of us can do everything, but each of us can do something. We can invite others to join us and as the movement for life grows we can have a united impact far beyond what any could have alone.

Two stories illustrate our potential for effecting change. One tells of a colony of monkeys in which only a few washed their food. Little by little over many days, others take up the food washing habit. At a certain point—the storyteller suggests it might be when "the hundredth monkey" begins to wash her food—the idea catches on and they all start food washing.[1] Something like that has often happened in human history. Ancient practices and customs like slavery, hostility between Christian denominations, and male dominance held sway over millions. Then a few began to question, doubt, and disbelieve. The brave among them then began to act in new ways. They were considered heretical, impractical, unpatriotic, irresponsible revolutionaries. But one day, after years of what seemed futile struggle, someone became "the hundredth monkey" and a new idea transformed an entire community. As we work for life, we dare to believe that one of us might be that "hundredth monkey."

The second illustration tells of a chickadee that asked a wild dove to tell the weight of a snowflake. "Nothing more than nothing," was the answer. "In that case," replied the chickadee, "I must tell you a marvelous story . . . I sat on the branch of a Fir. . . . Since I didn't have anything better to do, I counted the snowflakes settling on the twigs and needles of my branch. Their number was exactly 3,741,952. When the next snowflake dropped onto the branch—nothing more than nothing, as you say—the branch broke off." Then the chickadee flew away and the dove, who is reported to know something about peace, thought to herself, "Perhaps there is only one person's voice lacking for peace to come about in the world."[2] We often feel that the weight of our influence is "nothing more than nothing," but it is possible that one of us is snowflake number 3,741,953. Our voice may be the one needed "for peace to come about in the world" and for the institutions of death to be replaced by institutions of life.

Acquiescence or action?

We can imagine that we would have been courageous in opposing the Inquisition, child labor, slavery, and the Holocaust, but today's issues aren't as clear when we are in the midst of them. We don't like what is happening, but we fear controversy and keep silent. By passive acquiescence we affirm the institutions of death.

What is needed to motivate us to live as courageous stewards of life? Do we need to wait for more abortions and executions and until euthanasia has also become an established practice? Do we need an accidental nuclear explosion or even a "little nuclear war" to shock us out of psychic numbing and into sufficient revulsion to reverse the arms race?

Perhaps as less extreme shock therapy we should resume the draft, not with 18-year-olds, but with men in their 50s. We could also draft money for the military. The wealthy, whose money was conscripted by lottery, might be permitted to keep $100,000 in total assets. Since this would be a small sacrifice in comparison to that of young men drafted to kill and die for their country, the patriotic rich would surely be glad to serve in this way. Nevertheless, the power-brokers might be less inclined toward war if they had to fight it and pay for it themselves instead of calling on others to do the sacrificing while many of them grew richer from military spending.

It used to be said that alcoholics had to "hit bottom" in order to come to their senses. Now we know that they only need to "see bottom"—that is, to recognize the coming, but still avoidable, catastrophy before experiencing it. Does a world drunk on national pride, intoxicated with military power, and overindulging on the other institutions of death need to "hit bottom" before we come to our senses? Must we experience still greater disaster? Haven't we enough sense and sanity to "see bottom" and then choose new roads that lead to life?

Imagine what might happen if we and the other nations of the world began in even small measure to work and sacrifice for life as we now do in support of the institutions of death. Millions have risked their lives in warfare. How many of us are willing to risk even our reputations in working for peace and life in fullness for all God's children, including unborn, disabled, and infirm persons, and those condemned to die? It is not true that we create peace by preparing for war. Those who have prepared for war have almost always gotten war. If we want peace, we must prepare for peace. If we want life, we must work and sacrifice for life with the same loyalty and courage that are evident when nations go to war.

We must one day give account of our stewardship of life. Our sins of omission, as well as commission, will then be revealed. We can be sure that on that day we will be ashamed of our timidity and cowardice in the cause of Christ. Then none of us will be accused of having been too faithful to Christ and too courageous in our work and witness to sustain and ennoble God's wondrous gift of life.

While there is life, there is hope. Nuclear winter has not yet gripped our planet. There is still time to abolish the institutions of death. God who wills life is with us empowering us by the Holy Spirit to work for the fulfillment of every good purpose we see in Jesus. Therefore, Jesus' challenge is our own: "We must work the works of him who sent me while it is day; night comes, when no one can work" (John 9:4).

Specific challenges for stewards of life

As a reminder of our potential and possibilities, here is a list of specific challenges for stewards of life. It is suggestive, not exhaustive. Some items, such as to pray, are meant for us all; others may be appropriate only for some.

1. Trust in God.

"Set your troubled hearts at rest. Trust in God always; trust also in me" (John 14:1 NEB). Jesus reminds us that whatever we cannot do, we can always be sustained and empowered by the gracious assurance of God's mercy and power. As we look to Jesus, we are enabled to trust that whatever happens, God will be there to bless and use us. When the foundations of world and nation tremble we remain confident and "grateful for receiving a kingdom that cannot be shaken" (Heb. 12:28).

2. Surrender to God.

Someone confessed, "The best day of my life was when I resigned from being chair of the board of the universe." Letting God be God saves us from having to play at being God. We live poorly as make-believe gods, but amazingly well as authentic human beings loved and empowered by God. Surrendered to God, we refuse to live with unconditional surrender toward any human authority, and also refrain from demanding such surrender from any person or nation. God alone is worthy of unconditional surrender. When a nation demands such submission from a vanquished foe, it witnesses to its own idolatrous self-righteousness.

When yielded to God, our defeat by a victorious conqueror is not synonymous with surrender to evil. Military methods are only one form of resistance against tyranny and oppression. When guns and bombs fail, the "war" against evil has only begun. When surrendered to God we never surrender to evil; we fight on with the weapons of Christ. We do not attempt to defeat the devil with the devil's weapons or to overcome evil with evil, but to "overcome evil with good" (Rom. 12:21).

3. Pray.

"Our extremities are God's opportunities." Our weakness before the powerful institutions of death drives us to "pray constantly" (1 Thess. 5:17). In prayer we confess our own sins and not just the sins of others. We repent of our arrogance, pride, and greed. We give thanks for the mercy and promises of God. We intercede on behalf of all, including our enemies and generations yet unborn. In prayer of surrender we open our lives to the indwelling presence of God's life-giving Holy Spirit. We ask to be enabled to do by God's power what we are unable to do on our own.

4. Study the Bible.

Spend a half hour a day studying the Scriptures under the lordship of Christ. Start with the Gospels and the rest of the New Testament. Remember that Jesus is Lord of the Bible. Focus on what is revealed about Jesus and by Jesus. Note especially how Jesus is always pro-people and pro-life (see Mark 2:27 and John 10:10). Ponder passages such as the Sermon on the Plain in Luke

6, the Sermon on the Mount in Matthew 5–7, and the accounts of Jesus' encounter with the cross. Think about what the cross means for both our eternal salvation and for our daily living. Study the Old Testament in light of Christ and the great prophets. Let the Scriptures come alive as witness to the living God of love and power supremely revealed in Christ our Lord.

5. Study the witness of prophetic voices.

There are many differences among Christians concerning issues of life and death. The most helpful are those who combine an evangelical (in the historic sense of the word, meaning having an understanding of the gospel) perspective with a deep and wide commitment to justice, peace, and fullness of life for all of God's children. Leo Tolstoy's *The Kingdom of God and Peace Essays* and the writings of Mahatma Gandhi and Martin Luther King Jr. are becoming classics. *Nuclear Holocaust and Christian Hope* by Ronald Sider and Richard Taylor abounds in significant insights for Christian peacemakers. *Sojourner's* magazine and *The Other Side* speak from an evangelical perspective*.

6. Affirm pro-peace, pro-life movements as renewal of the Holy Spirit.

Charismatically renewed people have no monopoly on the Holy Spirit. God is on the side of life. Dare to believe and proclaim that the Holy Spirit—God at hand and God at work, God present and God powerful—is moving mightily to enable and invigorate all that makes for peace and fullness of life among God's children. Support every authentic manifestation of renewal in individuals and in the human family.

7. Study the state of the world.

Be among those Karl Barth described as living "with the Bible in one hand and the newspaper in the other." Become aware of what is involved in abortion, nuclear war, euthanasia, and capital

---

*Information concerning all references and resources to which this chapter refers is included in either the Notes or in Appendix 2.

punishment. Don't let talk of "termination of pregnancy" and "midget man missiles" lull you into unreality. Study Dr. Bernard Nathanson's *Aborting America.* Read *The Game of Disarmament* by Alva Myrdal, who received the Nobel Peace Prize, and Alan Geyer's *The Idea of Disarmament.* Question peace progaganda from both East and West that masks continued arms escalation. Study Lester Brown's *Building a Sustainable Society* and other writings. Learn how the arms race is robbing resources from the essential work of creating regenerative agriculture and sustainable ecological systems.

8. *Study and discuss together.*

Invite others to join in study and conversation. Plan Bible studies on alternatives to violence revealed in the teachings and life of Jesus. Have a book study in your congregation using this text and the questions for reflection and discussion included in Appendix 1, and a similar series using *Peaceways* by Charles Lutz and Jerry Folk. Hold adult and youth forums focusing on abortion, war, mercy killing, and the death penalty.

9. *Learn from the scientific/intellectual community.*

Read *The Bulletin of the Atomic Scientists,* which is written for intelligent lay readers, and become familiar with the Union of Concerned Scientists and groups like SANE (The Committee for a Sane Nuclear Policy) and The Council for a Liveable World. Learn from psychiatrists and international lawyers such as Robert Jay Lifton and Richard Falk who collaborated in writing *Indefensible Weapons: The Political and Psychological Case against Nuclearism.* Information from these sources will enable you to say no to arms escalation and "dream-world" proposals for defense such as the "Star Wars" strategy with the confidence that your position has the backing of many of the most brilliant and well-informed scientists and intellectual leaders in the United States and in the world. They will also help you to say yes to realistic alternatives to the continued militarization of the planet.

10. Learn from enlightened military leaders.

Support the work of the Center for Defense Information in Washington, D.C., which "supports a strong defense but opposes excessive expenditures for weapons and policies that increase the danger of nuclear war." The Center's leaders are retired admirals and generals. Their newsletter, *The Defense Monitor,* provides accurate information concerning the military strength of the United States and the Soviet Union, warns against the dangers of excessive militarism, and stresses the importance of non-military factors in the creation of national and global security. Remind all who still believe in military solutions to human problems of this statement from General Douglas MacArthur: "In the evolution of civilization, if it is to survive, all men [and women] cannot fail eventually to adopt Gandhi's belief that the process of mass applications of force to resolve contentious issues is fundamentally not only wrong, but contains within itself the germs of self-destruction."[3]

11. Celebrate life.

Pastors: plan worship services and sermons that affirm God's gift of life. When texts and themes express stewardship of life, speak to the issues of life and death, not from the perspective of a political party, but from the Scriptures understood in Christ. Lay people: encourage affirmation-of-life services and sermons. Be faithful to Christ and be stewards of life. Then any resulting controversy will relate to Christ and the Bible, not just to politics. When conflicts arise, always emphasize the common ground on which we stand together under the lordship of Christ.

12. Join a pro-life and a pro-peace group.

Seek out, support, and draw encouragement from your church's pro-life, pro-peace work. If you are Lutheran, join the Lutheran Peace Fellowship and Lutherans for Life. If you are a Roman Catholic, join Pax Christi USA and your local Respect Life work.

Many other denominations have similar groups committed to peace, life, and justice.

Consistently life-affirming people are unlikely to feel totally at home in either a pro-life or pro-peace group. You will share many convictions of each, but will differ with others. Don't let such differences keep you away. You can be a bridge between the pro-life and pro-peace movements. If such groups don't exist in your community, consider starting them yourself.

Also support organizations such as Prolifers for Survival, Feminists for Life, and Evangelicals for Social Action, which combine pro-peace, pro-life, pro-equality, and pro-justice concerns.

13. Practice peacemaking in your personal relationships.

Read *Getting to Yes* by Roger Fisher and William Ury. Learn commonsense methods of resolving personal conflicts peacefully. Think of how these principles can prevent violence in community and global conflicts.

14. Write and speak for life.

Share your convictions in letters to elected representatives and your local newspaper. Write often; express appreciation as well as criticism. Imagine the effect of the tons of letters that would arrive in Washington if every pro-life, pro-peace person were to write a letter today. In letter writing as in everything else, we should do that which would be beneficial if everyone did it. Invite friends and neighbors to your home for discussion of these issues. Speak out on these themes at your service or professional club or women's circle. If you are not a public speaker, have a video or film presentation.

15. Participate in the political process.

Vote for those who are most consistently life-affirming and who are more concerned about the next generation than the next election. Faithfulness to such criteria requires many difficult decisions. Candidates opposed to abortion may support the institutions of war and capital punishment, and vice versa. When consistently pro-life, we cannot decide on the basis of a single issue.

We should work for life through the political process, beginning with precinct caucuses. Consistently pro-life people will be uncomfortable with both the Republicans and Democrats. Both parties need to be challenged to affirm life and to deny the institutions of death.

16. Participate in rallies and marches for life.

Rallies and marches dramatize the depth and extent of pro-life convictions. When possible, hold a united demonstration for life in all its dimensions, but do not insist on participating only with people with whom you agree on everything. March and rally with those who are pro-life and pro-peace, even when you must do so separately. Don't retreat into isolation and ineffectiveness.

17. Examine your vocational commitment.

Does your daily work support an antilife institution? A pro-life person could not in good conscience be employed by an abortion clinic that performed unjustifiable abortions, or help build atomic bombs, or develop nerve gas. Because its tentacles spread so widely, many vocations are part of the military, industrial, scientific, academic complex. All who work in this vast arena must come to terms with their own consciences in this regard; none should carelessly avoid the issue. If we are working to prepare for unjustifiable warfare, there may be no alternative but to refuse to support it by our labor.

18. Consider conscientious objection.

Christians considering military service should be confronted with the moral issues long before the day of induction. These issues should be discussed in Sunday school, confirmation, and young-adult groups. We should not tell young people *what to think* but we should help them *to think* so that they will not drift thoughtlessly, through peer pressure or jingoistic propaganda, into

military service. Christians may never agree on all matters related
to violence and pacifism, but we can certainly agree that no Christian is justified in ignoring the witness of Jesus while making
choices related to life and death.

If it is sometimes wrong to participate in military industry and
military service, is it right for Christians to pay for these activities
with their taxes? If convinced that it would be wrong for me to
kill in war, is it right for me to, in effect, pay someone to kill
on my behalf? As noted earlier, serious confrontation with such
questions has prompted some pro-life people to refuse payment
of that portion of their taxes that is used for military purposes or
the lesser portion that is used for doomsday weapons. Others have
withheld a small, symbolic amount of their taxes as a token of
their opposition to war making. Some have likened such action
to throwing a single tea bag into the Boston harbor or sitting with
Rosa Parks for just five minutes at the front of the bus. Still others
have paid their taxes in full while enclosing a letter of protest.
Many are also working in support of the "National Campaign for
a Peace Tax Fund," which would legalize conscientious objection
to war-tax payments as well as in relation to military service. The
goal of this campaign is "a law permitting people morally opposed
to war to have the military part of their taxes allocated to peacemaking."

Those who choose such protest should complete their tax re-
turns in full. No claims for unauthorized deductions should be
made, and no "frivolous" comments should be written on the
return. A letter attached to the return should indicate the amount
of tax that is not being paid and the taxpayer's conscientious
convictions for choosing this action.

If the institutions of death continue to flourish, it may be necessary for conscientious pro-life people to engage in other acts
of nonviolent noncooperation in order to undermine their power.
Thankfully, we live in a democratic society and should exercise
every legal means before turning to acts of civil disobedience.

But as persons controlled by the love of Christ, we cannot fore-close the possibility of such action. If our nation blunders into a nuclear holocaust, it will be small comfort to report that it was done by a democratic society. We remember that Hitler was voted into power and do well to ponder someone's observation that "The kind of leader who could lead the United States down the road of fascism and war will not rant and rave like Adolf Hitler but will sound much more like Arthur Godfrey," a well-known mid-century radio personality. In America as in every society, eternal vigilance is essential for freedom and for life.

19. Support a national peace academy.

We spend billions on basic military training and in support of the national military academies and war colleges, but next to nothing on learning the arts of peacemaking. Proposals calling for the establishment of a National Academy of Peace and Conflict Resolution are regularly introduced in Congress, and some min-imal steps toward their implementation have been taken. Urge your senators and representatives to back this effort. If the day is ever to come when "nation shall not lift up sword against nation, neither shall they learn war any more" (Isa. 2:4) we must not only stop learning war but must start learning peace.

20. Learn to think and act globally.

The Russell-Einstein manifesto stated: "Remember your hu-manity and forget the rest."[4] For help in living with a global perspective, become a member of Global Education Associates and the World Federalists. To glimpse the possibility of a global security system, read Emery Reves's *The Anatomy of Peace* and Clark and Sohn's *Introduction to World Peace through World Law*. Become acquainted with journals such as *Transnational Per-spectives, The Inter Dependent,* and *World Press Review*.

21. Become an advocate of civilian-based, nonviolent defense.

Study the works of Gene Sharp on *The Politics of Nonviolent Action* and *National Security through Civilian-Based Defense.* Read *War without Weapons* by Anders Boserup and Andrew Mack. Ponder the possibilities and problems of defeating aggressors and overcoming oppressors by nonviolent noncooperation. Urge our political leaders to follow Sweden's example in designating a portion of the military budget for study and training in civilian-based defense. Become familiar with the Association for Transarmament Studies, and encourage discussion of these methods in church and community groups.

22. If it fits you, join a special-interest peace group.

If you are a medical doctor, nurse, or health-care provider, join Physicians for Social Responsibility. If an educator, join Educators for Social Responsibility. Women: join Women against Military Madness. Similar groups exist for lawyers, scientists, and others of many professions. If there is none that fits you, consider starting one.

23. Work to strengthen and reform the United Nations.

The UN is an essential but flawed organization; without it the world would be a more dangerous place. The Secretary General of the United Nations recently stated that the annual expenditure of the UN is only two-thirds of the budget of the New York City police department and only one-third the cost of a single Trident submarine. Those who complain of what it costs us to belong to the UN should also be reminded that because its headquarters is in New York City, we make more from what the UN contributes to the economy of New York than we provide as our nation's share of its support. Study Richard Hudson's proposal for a "binding triad" in the voting system of the United Nations and plans for UN reform, such as those of Clark and Sohn noted earlier, which seek to give the United Nations authority appropriate to its responsibility.

24. Support groups committed to life.

Give your support to groups such as the National Right to Life Committee and the many state and local organizations committed to decreasing unjustifiable abortion, and to organizations such as The National Coalition against the Death Penalty and Amnesty International that stand in opposition to capital punishment and the torture and unjust treatment of prisoners.

25. Visit the homelands of our "enemies."

Take a trip to the Soviet Union. Visit places such as Central America, the Middle East, South Africa, and China. Encourage massive educational, economic, and cultural exchanges between countries whose governments are at enmity with each other. Discover for yourself, and encourage others to discover, that there are human beings who yearn for peace, freedom, and justice in every country on earth.

26. Risk being considered a fanatic for peace and for life.

Don't become a fanatic, but risk being considered one. There is a fanatic fringe around every creative movement in human history. There are pro-peace, pro-life, and pro-feminist fanatics, and a host of fanatics claiming to be the only true followers of Jesus. It has been rightly observed that "when a light goes on the bugs often gather around the light." Some support the right causes for the wrong reasons. Don't let them keep you from making a clear and rational witness for life and for peace. Jesus risked his reputation by associating with tax collectors and sinners; risk yours by association with people with whom you agree on at least one vital matter while disagreeing on others. Let God and future generations, and not current public opinion, be the judge of your actions.

Søren Kierkegaard tells of a clown who discovered the theater to be on fire. He raced on stage screaming, "Fire! Fire!" The audience thought it part of his act. The more he cried, "Fire!" the more they laughed and applauded his performance. And so, in spite of being warned, they perished in the fire.

When we shout our warnings against the institutions of death, some will hear us as the crowd heard that clown. They may laugh, or even applaud, but not take us seriously. We are, therefore, challenged to match our intensity with calm and persuasive rationality that will inspire others to act appropriately.

27. Learn from and support the peace churches and caring agencies.

Become acquainted with the Quakers, Mennonites, and Church of the Brethren. Support the work of the American Friends Service Committee and The Fellowship of Reconciliation. Read the Friends' newsletter and *Fellowship* magazine. Learn about "militant nonviolence." Contribute to agencies for global development and food assistance. Support organizations like Bread for the World that work for justice, peace, and fullness of life for all people.

28. Support the work of crisis pregnancy centers.

These centers, like Birthright, seek to provide responsible alternatives to abortion for those struggling with problems of unwanted pregnancy. Become acquainted with books such as *Should I Keep My Baby?* by Martha Zimmerman, written specifically for women in this situation.

29. Teach your children to be pro-life and pro-peace.

Rambo dolls and other war toys that teach violence and irreverence for life are inappropriate gifts for children. When we celebrate the birth of the "Prince of Peace" (Isa. 9:6) and "Author of life" (Acts 3:15), teach your children that those who lack the strength and intelligence to solve conflicts by nonviolent means are weak and foolish. Teach them that Jesus is strong and that people like Rambo and Hitler are sick and sinful in their attitudes and actions. Tell your children about Gandhi, Martin Luther King Jr., Albert Schweitzer, Albert Einstein, and others who have had the wisdom and strength to renounce violence and affirm the intelligent resolution of human conflict.

30. Remember—we've only just begun.

On his 70th birthday, one man observed that his life covered 1/100th of recorded human history. All who live to be 100 will have experienced 1/20th of all Christian history. When it seems that humanity has failed to create a just society with peace and fullness of life for all God's children, remember our youthfulness. Humanity is still in its childhood, or at least not beyond its adolescence. We've only just begun to solve the problems of living together.

We are tempted to disparage the dinosaurs who were "too dumb" to survive, but we had best not be too proud. There is evidence that dinosaurs dominated life on this planet for 75 million years! If humanity is to survive for the next 1000 years (let alone 75,000 times 1000) it is imperative that we begin at once to destroy the old institutions of death and to create new institutions of life.

Each of us needs the satisfaction of completing short-term tasks, but we also need to be committed to some great purposes that will not be accomplished in our lifetimes. We are to work today to help enable meaningful and joyful life on this planet for hundreds of generations yet to be.

Summing up

Ashley Montague has observed that, "There are many millions of Christians but very few followers of Jesus." When Gandhi was asked to name the greatest enemy of Jesus in the world, he answered, "Christianity!" These statements may be exaggerated, but there is enough truth in each of them to prompt our thought, self-examination, confession, and repentance. It is easier to be an adherent of "Christianity" than a faithful follower of Jesus. At best, our "Christianity" is a sign of our discipleship; at worst it is only a substitute for it.

In *The Politics of Jesus,* John Howard Yoder points to our idolatrous dependence on material goods and our use of violence as two of the most glaring examples of our disharmony with the way of Jesus. These two, as we have noted, are closely related. Having too much to defend, we easily become excessively preoccupied with preserving it, even with violent means. Similarly, in defending our rights we often ignore and even deny the rights of others and especially those of the weakest among us—the unborn, infirm, disabled, and imprisoned persons.

When all is said and done, it doesn't much matter whether you agree with me or John Howard Yoder, but it matters mightily whether we who call ourselves Christians are living in harmony with the life and teaching of Jesus. For centuries, many Christians lived in conformity with slavery and out of tune with Jesus' teaching to love our neighbors, not only as we love ourselves but even as Jesus loves us. Most Christians are still living in conformity with the violent world and contrary to the teaching and example of the Prince of Peace. The challenges of the present crisis and the voice of Jesus unite in calling us to repent and turn from the old ways of death to new ways that make for life. In Christ we are now called to replace oppression with justice, accusation with reconciliation, tribalism with globalism, vengeance with rehabilitation, killing with caring, the sword with the cross, and, in all things, death with life. With ears of faith we hear the voice of the living and life-giving Christ joining with the voices of all God's children who yearn for life. These voices call us to be pro-life/pro-peace people in all our living.

Notes

Chapter 1

1. Adin Ballou, "How Many Does it Take?" quoted in Leo Tolstoy, *The Kingdom of God and Peace Essays* (London: Oxford, 1974), p. 14.

Chapter 4

1. From *Christianity and Crisis,* 45 (April 15, 1985): 123.
2. Elenore Hamilton, *Sex With Love: A Guide for Young People* (Boston: Beacon, 1978) p. 39.
3. Bernard N. Nathanson, M.D. with Richard N. Ostling, *Aborting America* (Garden City, N.Y.: Doubleday, 1979), p. 194.

Chapter 5

1. Ralph E. Lap, "The Einstein Letter that Started it All," *New York Times Magazine,* August 2, 1964, p. 54.
2. Ronald W. Clark, *Einstein, the Life and Times* (New York: World, 1971), p. 591.
3. Harry Emerson Fosdick, "Putting Christ into Uniform," sermon preached at Riverside Church, New York City, Nov. 12, 1939, and published by the church in pamphlet form, pp. 12-13.
4. Dorothee Soelle, *The Arms Race Kills Even without War* (Philadelphia: Fortress, 1983).
5. Sydney J. Harris, *Pieces of Eight* (Boston: Houghton Mifflin, 1982), p. 47.

6. Roger Fisher, "Preventing Nuclear War," *Bulletin of the Atomic Scientists,* March 1981, p. 16.

7. Norman Cousins, *Human Options* (New York: Norton, 1981), p. 64.

8. M. Scott Peck, *People of the Lie* (New York: Simon & Schuster, 1983), p. 246.

9. Gene Sharp, *Social Power and Political Freedom* (Boston: Porter Sargent, 1980), pp. 246-247.

10. Colin Morris, *Unyoung—Uncolored—Unpoor* (Nashville: Abingdon, 1969), pp. 111-113.

11. Omar Bradley, speech quoted in Gwyn Prins, ed., *Defended to Death* (London: Pelican, 1983), pp. 294-295.

12. Martin Luther King Jr., "Letter from Birmingham Jail," April 16, 1963, from *Why We Can't Wait* (New York: Harper & Row, 1964), p. 89.

13. Harry Emerson Fosdick, *Riverside Sermons* (New York: Harper and Brothers, 1958), pp. 349-352, copyright © 1958 by Harry Emerson Fosdick. Reprinted by permission of Harper & Row, Publishers, Inc. and William Collins Sons & Co. Ltd.

Chapter 8

1. Ken Kesey Jr., *The Hundredth Monkey* (Coos Bay, Ore.: Vision, 1982), pp. 11-16.

2. Ronald J. Sider and Richard K. Taylor, *Nuclear Holocaust and Christian Hope* (Ramsey, N.J.: Paulist, 1982), p. 162.

3. "Conscience and Military Tax Campaign—U.S. Newsletter (Bellport, N.Y.) Fall 1984.

4. From *Bulletin of the Atomic Scientists,* November 1955, pp. 236-237.

Appendix 1

QUESTIONS AND SUGGESTIONS FOR REFLECTION AND DISCUSSION

These questions and suggestions are intended to stimulate personal reflection and group discussion and are especially for use by congregational forums and study groups. An eight-week series might be structured as follows. In shorter series some sessions can be combined.

Session 1 (Preface and Chapters 1–3)

1. What are the main differences between the "pro-life" and "pro-peace" people in your community? Where do you see yourself?
2. What does it mean to be "pro-life"? "pro-peace"? to be a pacifist?
3. What gives life value? What is the meaning of "reverence for life"?
4. List implications of Jesus' coming that we "may have life, and may have it in all its fullness" (John 10:10 NEB) and discuss ways in which Jesus was consistently life affirming.
5. Compare and contrast the implications of loving our neighbors *as we love ourselves* and loving them *even as Jesus loves us*.

6. Discuss ways in which the Old Testament rejects idolatrous dependence on military power. In what sense does the New Testament supersede Old Testament teaching?

7. How large does a group have to be before it can set aside the personal prohibition against killing? Was Tolstoy correct in questioning this distinction? Why? Why not?

8. What does it mean to be a steward of life? How are we to exercise this stewardship?

9. What are we to do when one life threatens another? How do we determine the value of one life over another?

10. What is the difference between taking life in tragic, exceptional circumstances and claiming an inherent right to do so?

11. Discuss the differences between the exceptional and institutional taking of life. List examples of situations in which the exception has become the rule. Is this morally justifiable? Why? Why not?

12. Discuss the strengths and weaknesses of an absolute refusal to take life in any circumstances.

Session 2 (Abortion and Its Pro-life Alternatives)

1. Discuss the validity, or lack thereof, of comparing legalization of abortion with the Dred Scott decision and Hitler's Holocaust.

2. On what common ground can "pro-life" and "pro-choice" advocates stand together?

3. When does human life begin? Are there stages of development during which the unborn are more fully human than at others? When are we fully human?

4. What is the significance, if any, of implantation, brain birth, and viability in determining the value of the unborn?

5. Do you agree that the *Roe* v. *Wade* decision, in effect, institutionalized and established abortion on demand during most of pregnancy? Why? Why not?

6. Why is it right, or wrong, for feminists and liberals to affirm a woman's "right" to an abortion?

7. Should fathers have any say in determining the fate of their unborn children? Why? Why not?

8. List and discuss criteria for justifiable versus unjustifiable abortion. Should there be different criteria for preventing implantation and killing the unborn prior to brain birth? Why? Why not? What are we to do when there is doubt concerning the humanness of the unborn?

9. Discuss ways in which the use of expressions such as "termination of pregnancy" and "the products of conception" influence our attitudes toward abortion.

10. Evaluate alternatives to abortion, including sex education, contraception, sexual satisfaction apart from intercourse, and adoption.

11. What is the difference between crime and sin? Should all sinful abortions be legally classified as crimes? Why? Why not?

12. Do women have a moral and legal "right" to have an abortion? Should abortion laws be more permissive during early pregnancy than later? Evaluate proposals for the legal prohibition or restriction of abortion. When is an abortion morally justifiable? legally justifiable?

13. What are the limits of our personal freedom? When is it right, or wrong, to impose our personal morality on others?

14. Does a global population explosion justify the acceptance, or advocacy, of easily obtainable abortion? Why? Why not?

15. What more could be done under existing legal structures to reduce the number of morally unjustifiable abortions?

Session 3 (War and Its Pro-life Alternatives)
Part 1: Background Considerations

1. What challenges does present military technology present to us as human beings? as Christians?

2. Do you agree that the military should oppose the arms race because the development of "doomsday weapons" has "ruined war"? Why? Why not?

3. Discuss Albert Einstein's statement, "The unleashed power of the atom has changed everything save our modes of thinking, and we thus drift toward unparalleled catastrophe." Do you agree? Why? Why not?

4. What needs to happen in order to bring our thinking and acting in line with the realities of military technology? with Christian morality?

5. Compare and contrast the sacrifice of Christ on the cross with that of soldiers in battle.

6. Evaluate the criteria for justifiable versus unjustifiable warfare. Is it ever justifiable for Christians to go to war against each other? Is the use of nuclear weapons ever justifiable?

7. Is it justifiable for Christians to help build weapons of mass destruction and to threaten their use?

8. When is it justifiable for Christians to serve in the military? Discuss differences between "total" and "selective" conscientious objection. Does just/unjust war thinking require selective conscientious objection? Why? Why not?

9. What are the responsibilities of Christian military chaplains in clarifying the moral issues related to war making? Should they have freedom to speak against some policies and to counsel disobedience to orders considered sinful? Why? Why not?

10. Discuss the morality of deterrence based on the threat of "massive, assured destruction." If such deterrence fails, is retaliation justifiable? Why? Why not?

11. Discuss the morality of "counterforce" nuclear weapons targeted against military sites versus that of "countervalue" weapons targeted against cities. What are the implications of each?

12. Evaluate the morality of the arms race itself. To what extent is it true that "the arms race kills even without war"?

13. Compare the risks of continuing the arms race with the risks of stopping it. What do you think the world will be like 100, 500, and 1000 years from now?

14. What is the difference between the abolition of the institution of war and the abolition of conflict? Can we abolish the one without eliminating the other? Why? Why not?

Session 4 (War and Its Pro-life Alternatives)
Part 2: Peace through Justice, Reconciliation, and Global Security

1. In what ways does Jesus challenge us to find alternatives to war? Why haven't most Christians taken these teachings seriously? What would happen if we did?

2. What is the relationship between working for peace and working for justice? In what ways is injustice at the root of war, and justice the foundation of peace?

3. To what extent do we judge ourselves by our motives and others by their actions? Share examples of ways in which noble intentions have failed to guarantee laudable actions and positive results.

4. Which is more likely to help create lasting security: (1) increased expenditure for armaments, or (2) increased developmental assistance to hungry and oppressed people? Why? To what extent does our national and global security depend on economic, social, political, and moral factors rather than only on military power?

5. What is at the center of a Christian "ministry of reconciliation"? What are its implications for personal and global relationships?

6. What is the difference between being a "peacemaker" and a "peacekeeper"? How are we Christians to be "in the reconciliation business"?

7. Which involves greater risk: (a) increased military spending, or (b) diverting money from the military for increased training in negotiation and reconciliation? Why?

8. Study the story of Rehoboam in 1 Kings 12:1-20 and discuss the lessons it has to teach us.

9. Discuss ways in which we tend to dehumanize and demonize our enemies. What kinds of "final solutions" become thinkable when we see our enemies as the incarnation of all evil?

10. What might be the benefits of a massive exchange of U.S. and Soviet citizens and of having the relatives of our national leaders living in the other country? What else can we do to discover human beings among our enemies?

11. Do you agree that "the world's great need is not for more military specialists but for human relations experts who are wise in the arts of reconciliation and negotiation"? Why? Why not?

12. Discuss and evaluate proposals for a total test ban, a nuclear freeze, unilateral steps toward mutual disarmament, and annual summit conferences. What are the risks and potential benefits of these actions?

13. To what extent are Christians to live with a sense of global citizenship? What is proper national patriotism? What is improper? When does patriotism become idolatrous?

14. In what sense is all war civil war? Discuss the "modest proposal for peace—that the Christians of the world stop killing each other."

15. Do you agree that "There can no longer be lasting national security without global security" and that the independently secure nation-state is now "obsolete"? Why? Why not? What is now required for national and global security?

16. Discuss the problems and possibilities of a global security system. What powers would it require? How should it be limited? How should the United Nations be improved?

17. Discuss the differences between police power and military power. What is the purpose of each? How do they operate in practice? Can we affirm the one while rejecting the other?

18. What steps can we take today to make global security possible tomorrow? As citizens with global perspective, what responsibility do we Christians have in this regard?

Session 5 (War and Its Pro-life Alternatives)
Part 3: Peace through the Way of the Cross

1. In addition to witnessing to our redemption and salvation what does the cross of Christ mean for our daily living? How does the cross witness to "the cost of Christ-like living in a sinful world"?

2. Discuss the statements of Jesus in Matt. 26:52 and Luke 22:51. What would happen if the majority of Christians were to obey these teachings?

3. If it was justifiable for Christians to go to war *against* Hitler, was it unjustifiable for other Christians to go to war *for* Hitler? Why? Why not? What would have happened if millions of Christians had refused to cooperate with Hitler?

4. From whom do all leaders receive their power? What does this mean for the potential power of people to topple tyrants and to deter and overcome conquerors?

5. How does military experience enhance or degrade personal morality? Do you agree that Hitler's Holocaust would have been impossible apart from the demoralizing impact of war? Why? Why not?
6. What could be done to increase training in nonviolence? Why don't governments provide such training?
7. Discuss the differences between spiteful and loving nonviolent action. How can spiteful and loving protesters work together?
8. Discuss the capabilities and limitations of "civilian-based defense." What might it accomplish? What harm can't it do? When is nonviolent "defeat" preferable to violent "victory"?
9. When does divine obedience necessitate civil disobedience? When is it acceptable? Discuss the meaning of Rom. 13:1-10 and Mark 12:13-17. Do you agree with Colin Morris' interpretation of Mark 12:17 that Jesus' answer was "a resounding 'No!' " to payment of taxes to Caesar? Why? Why not?
10. In what ways are we sometimes guilty of "idolatrous polytheism"? In addition to worshiping the true God, what false gods are we tempted to worship? Do we trust the true God for eternal salvation and false gods for temporal salvation?
11. Discuss the differences between the one jealous God and the many nonjealous gods. Why do our false gods often encourage us to worship the true God?
12. Discuss the sins of excessive militarism. How are we to repent of these sins? How do we "produce fruit in keeping with [such] repentance" (Matt. 3:8 NIV)?
13. How does what we have discussed in this session relate to Luke 9:23-24? What is the significance of living the way of the cross "daily"? Do nations as well as individuals "lose" their lives when their chief aim is to "save" them? How might a nation "save" its own life and the lives of other nations by losing it?

Session 6 (Mercy Killing and Its Pro-life Alternatives)

1. When does medical technology become a curse instead of a blessing?
2. In what ways does modern medicine make consideration of mercy killing less necessary than previously? more necessary?

3. Do you agree with the widespread acceptance of passive euthanasia? Why? Why not? What are the dangers of such acceptance?

4. Do you believe that legal and cultural acceptance of war, abortion, and capital punishment makes it easier for a society to also accept mercy killing? Why? Why not?

5. When is passive euthanasia justifiable? unjustifiable?

6. Who should have major responsibility for "pulling the plug"? the patient? the family? the doctor? Why?

7. To what extent should a patient's wishes concerning euthanasia be respected? When is it justifiable to refuse to cooperate with a patient's desire to die?

8. Should handicapped newborns receive greater, less, or the same legal protection from mercy killing as the elderly? Why? When, if ever, is infanticide justifiable?

9. In what circumstances might active euthanasia be more moral than passive? Does this justify the legalization of active euthanasia? Why? Why not? Discuss the dangers of this "slippery slope."

10. Discuss the emotional and economic factors related to euthanasia. What influence should feelings and money have on these decisions?

11. What steps should be taken to prevent economic considerations from pressuring us toward easy euthanasia? What is the role of the church in this regard? the government?

12. Discuss and evaluate positive, pro-life alternatives to unjustifiable euthanasia. What should we be doing to create and maintain these alternatives?

Session 7 (The Death Penalty and Its Pro-life Alternatives)

1. List and discuss examples of situations in which you believe capital punishment to be justifiable.

2. Evaluate the practice of capital punishment in the Old Testament. Study and discuss Lev. 20:10 and Deut. 22:22. Are these texts applicable to Christians today? Why? Why not? Study and discuss John 8:3-11. What does Jesus' response to the statement that "in the law Moses commanded us to stone such" teach us about his attitude toward some Old Testament teachings?

3. If only those who are "without sin" are to cast the first stone, how can Christians practice and support capital punishment? What would happen if Christians were to follow this teaching?

4. If it is true that "ignorance of the law is no excuse," what is the meaning of Jesus' prayer "Father, forgive them; for they know not what they do" (Luke 23:34)? What is the relationship between such forgiveness and the practice of capital punishment?

5. Study Rom. 12:19. What is the place of vengeance in the Christian life?

6. To what extent does capital punishment deter crime? If significant deterrent effect could be established, does this automatically justify the use of the death penalty? Why? Why not? In what situations might the existence of capital punishment motivate someone to murder?

7. How does capital punishment teach reverence for life? How does it teach irreverence for life?

8. Compare and contrast deterring thievery by cutting off the hands of thieves and deterring murder by killing murderers. Which is more humane? more barbaric?

9. Do you agree that capital punishment discriminates against the poor, minorities, and men? Why? Why not?

10. Of what significance is the possibility of execution of the innocent on the practice of capital punishment?

11. Discuss economic factors related to the use of the death penalty. Is execution always cheaper than incarceration? To what extent should money matters be determinative in this regard?

12. Discuss pro-life alternatives to capital punishment. In what circumstances is life imprisonment without possibility of parole justifiable? What is the purpose of prisons? Discuss possibilities for prison reform. What is the experience of other states and countries in this regard?

13. To what extent do our citizens have a right to own a gun? Is gun control an effective means of reducing homicide? Why? Why not?

14. Since alcohol and drugs are involved in many crimes and murders, should there be greater restrictions on their use and advertising?

Should it be permissible to advertise drugs and alcohol as means of achieving peace and joy? Why? Why not?

15. Which countries execute the most criminals? Are these good models for us to follow? Why? Why not? Do you agree with Amnesty International that the imposition of the death penalty is "a violation of fundamental human rights"? Why? Why not?

16. Do you agree that capital punishment is "an issue over which Christians can reasonably disagree"? Why? Why not? What should Christians universally oppose? What should they universally favor?

Session 8 (What One Person Can Do)

1. Review the illustrations of "the hundredth monkey" and the "chickadee and the weight of a snowflake." Do you agree with the implications of these stories concerning our potential influence? Why? Why not?

2. Why is it easier to imagine ourselves acting bravely in times of past moral crisis than for us to act decisively today? What is required to motivate us to act courageously today? Do you agree that "a little nuclear war" may be necessary to shock us out of our psychic numbing? Should we start drafting men (and women) at age 50 and also start "drafting" money?

3. Review each of the "specific challenges for stewards of life" presented in Chapter 8. Select several for discussion and suggest others. Which have the highest priority? What can we do now to begin to act on them?

4. How true is Ashley Montague's statement that "There are many millions of Christians but very few followers of Jesus," and Gandhi's that "Christianity is the greatest enemy of Jesus in the world"? If there is any truth in these statements, how are we to respond?

5. Summarize ways in which the Christian church has failed to be consistently pro-life. How can we be more consistently life-affirming in all our living?

6. Review the "References and Resources for Further Study and Mutual Support" listed in Appendix 2. What do these suggest for further study, discussion, and action?

7. Share what you—as individuals, as a group, and as a congregation—plan to do in response to having participated in this study/discussion series.

Appendix 2

References and Resources for Further Study and Mutual Support

Books

Andrusko, Dave, ed. *To Rescue the Future: The Pro-Life Movement in the 1980s.* Toronto: Life Cycle Books, 1983.

Aukerman, Dale. *Darkening Valley: A Biblical Perspective on Nuclear War.* Minneapolis: Winston-Seabury, 1981.

Bainton, Roland. *Christian Attitudes toward War and Peace.* Nashville: Abingdon, 1979.

Beachy, Duane. *Faith in a Nuclear Age: A Christian Response to War.* Scottdale, Pa.: Herald, 1983.

Bloomfield, Lincoln P. *The Power to Keep Peace, Today and in a World without War.* Berkeley, Calif.: World without War Council Publications, 1971.

Boserup, Anders and Mack, Andrew. *War without Weapons: Non-Violence in National Defense.* New York: Schocken, 1975.

Brown, Lester R. *Building a Sustainable Society.* New York: Norton, 1981.

Brown, Lester R. *The State of the World, 1985: A Worldwatch Institute Report on Progress toward a Sustainable Society.* New York: Norton, 1985.

Brown, Robert McAfee. *Making Peace in the Global Village.* Philadelphia: Westminster, 1981.

Burns, Weston H., ed. *Toward Nuclear Disarmament and Global Security: A Search for Alternatives.* Studies on a Just World Order Series, no. 4. Boulder, Col.: Westview, 1984.

Camus, Albert. *Neither Victims Nor Executioners.* New York: Continuum, 1980.

Clark, Grenville and Sohn, Lewis. *Introduction to World Peace through World Law,* Chicago: World without War Publications, 1984.

Clark, Greenville. *World Peace through World Law. Two Alternative Plans.* 3rd. ed. Ann Arbor, Mich.: Books on Demand (imprint of Univ. Microfilms International).

Cleveland, Harlan. *The Third Try at World Order: U.S. Policy for an Interdependent World.* New York: Aspen Institute for Humanistic Studies, 1977.

Craigie, Peter C. *War in the Old Testament.* Grand Rapids, Mich.: Eerdmans, 1979.

Douglas, James W. *The Nonviolent Cross: A Theology of Revolution and Peace.* New York: Macmillan, 1969. (Out of print.)

Dyson, Freeman. *Weapons and Hope.* New York: Harper & Row, 1985.

Erlander, Daniel. *By Faith Alone: A Lutheran Looks at the Bomb.* Chelan, Wash.: Holden Village Press, 1982.

Fisher, Roger and Ury, William. *Getting to Yes: Negotiating Agreement without Giving In.* Boston: Houghton Mifflin, 1981.

Freudenberger, C. Dean. *Food for Tomorrow?* Minneapolis: Augsburg, 1984.

Galtung, Johan. *The True Worlds: A Transnational Experience.* New York: Free Press, 1981.

Gandhi, Mahatma. *All Men Are Brothers.* Weare, N.H.: Greenleaf, 1982.

Gandhi, Mahatma. *An Autobiography or the Story of My Experiments with Truth.* Weare, N.H.: Greenleaf, 1982.

Gandhi, Mahatma. *The Message of Jesus Christ.* Bombay, India: Bharatiya Vidya Bhavan, 1971.

Gandhi, Mahatma. *Non-violent Resistance.* New York: Schocken, 1983.

Garton, Jean Staker. *Who Broke the Baby?* Minneapolis: Bethany, 1979.

Geyer, Alan. *The Idea of Disarmament: Rethinking the Unthinkable.* Elgin, Ill.: Brethren, 1982.

Grenier-Sweet, Gail. *Pro-Life Feminism: Different Voices.* Toronto: Life Cycle Books, 1985.

Kennan, George. *The Nuclear Delusion: Soviet-American Relations in the Atomic Age.* New York: Pantheon, 1982.

Levicoff, Steve. *Building Bridges: The Prolife Movement and the Peace Movement.* Eagleville, Pa.: Toviah Press, 1982.

Lifton, Robert Jay and Falk, Richard. *Indefensible Weapons: The Political and Psychological Case against Nuclearism.* New York: Basic, 1982.

Lifton, Robert Jay and Humphrey, Nicholas, eds. *In a Dark Time! Images for Survival.* Cambridge, Mass.: Harvard, 1984.

Lutz, Charles P. and Folk, Jerry L. *Peaceways.* Minneapolis: Augsburg, 1983.

Macgregor, G.H.C. *The New Testament Basis of Pacifism* and *The Relevance of an Impossible Ideal: An Answer to the Views of Reinhold Niebuhr.* Nyack, N.Y.: Fellowship Publications, 1954. (Out of print.)

McSorley, Richard. *New Testament Basis of Peacemaking.* Scottdale, Pa.: Herald Press, 1985.

Marx, Paul. *Euthanasia: Death without Dignity.* St. John's Abbey, Collegeville, Minn.: Liturgical Press, 1978.

Merton, Thomas. *Faith and Violence: Christian Teaching and Christian Practice.* Notre Dame, Ind.: Notre Dame, 1968.

Merton, Thomas, ed. *Gandhi on Non-Violence: Selected Texts from Gandhi's ''Non-Violence in Peace and War.''* New York: New Directions, 1965.

Mische, Gerald and Patricia. *Toward a Human World Order: Beyond the National Security Straitjacket.* Ramsey, N.J.: Paulist, 1977.

Mische, Patricia M. *Star Wars and the State of Our Souls: Deciding the Future of Planet Earth.* Minneapolis: Winston, 1984.

Myrdal, Alva. *The Game of Disarmament: How the United States and Russia Run the Arms Race.* New York: Pantheon, 1982.

Nathanson, Bernard N. and Ostling, Richard N. *Aborting America.* New York: Pinnacle, 1981.

Nelson, Jack A. *Hunger for Justice: The Politics of Food and Faith.* Maryknoll, N.Y.: Orbis, 1980.

Noonan, John T. Jr. *A Private Choice: Abortion in America in the Seventies.* New York: Free Press, 1979.

Nuttall, Geoffrey. *Christian Pacifism in History.* Berkeley, Calif.: World without War Council, 1958.

Osgood, Charles E. *An Alternative to War or Surrender.* Urbana, Ill.: Univ. of Illinois, 1962. (Out of print.)

Peachy, Lorne J. *How to Teach Peace to Children.* Scottdale, Pa.: Herald, 1981.

Powell, John. *Abortion: The Silent Holocaust.* Allen, Tex.: Argus, 1981.

Reves, Emery. *The Anatomy of Peace.* Gloucester, Mass.: Peter Smith, 1969.

Schell, Jonathan. *The Abolition.* New York: Knopf, 1984.

Schell, Jonathan. *The Fate of the Earth.* New York: Knopf, 1982.

Schneider, Edward D., ed. *Questions about the Beginnings of Life: Christian Appraisals of Seven Bioethical Issues.* Minneapolis: Augsburg, 1985.

Schramm, John and Mary. *Things That Make for Peace.* Minneapolis: Augsburg, 1976.

Sharp, Gene. *Gandhi as a Political Strategist, with Essays on Ethics and Politics.* Boston: Porter Sargent, 1979.

Sharp, Gene. *Making Europe Unconquerable: The Potential of Civilian-Based Deterrence and Defense.* London & Philadelphia: Taylor and Francis, 1985.

Sharp, Gene. *National Security through Civilian-Based Defense.* Omaha, Neb.: The Association for Transarmament Studies, 1985.

Sharp, Gene. *The Politics of Nonviolent Action.* Paperback in three volumes: (1) *Power and Struggle,* (2) *The Methods of Nonviolent Action,* and (3) *The Dynamics of Nonviolent Action.* Boston: Porter Sargent, 1974.

Sharp, Gene. *Social Power and Political Freedom*. Boston: Porter Sargent, 1980.

Sibley, Mulford Q. *The Quiet Battle: Writings on the Theory and Practice of Non-violent Resistance*. Boston: Beacon Press, 1963. (Out of print.)

Sider, Ronald J. *Christ and Violence*. Scottdale, Penn.: Herald, 1979.

Sider, Ronald J. and Taylor, Richard K. *Nuclear Holocaust and Christian Hope: A Book for Christian Peacemakers*. Downers Grove, Ill.: Inter-Varsity, 1982.

Soelle, Dorothee. *The Arms Race Kills Even without War.* Philadelphia: Fortress, 1983.

Soelle, Dorothee. *Of War and Love*. Maryknoll, N.Y.: Orbis Books, 1983.

Tolstoy, Leo. *The Kingdom of God and Peace Essays*. London: Oxford University Press, World Classics Reprint, 1974. (Out of print.)

Tuchman, Barbara W. *The March of Folly: From Troy to Vietnam*. New York: Knopf, 1984.

Van Doren, Carl. *The Great Rehearsal: The Story of the Making and Ratifying of the Constitution of the United States*. New York: Viking, 1948 and 1986.

Van Ornum, William and Wicker, Mary. *Talking to Children about Nuclear War.* New York: Crossroad, 1984.

Wallis, Jim. *The Call to Conversion: Recovering the Gospel for These Times*. San Francisco: Harper & Row, 1983.

Wallis, Jim, ed. *Waging Peace: A Handbook for the Struggle against Nuclear Arms*. San Francisco: Harper & Row, 1982.

Wells, Donald A. *The War Myth: The Rationalization of War-Making in Western Thought with an Analysis of the Human Dilemmas That Cause War.* New York: Pegasus—Western, 1967. (Out of print.)

Willke, J. C. *Handbook on Abortion*. Cincinnati: Hayes, 1979.

Yoder, John Howard. *Nevertheless: The Varieties and Shortcomings of Religious Pacifism*. Scottdale, Pa.: Herald, 1972.

Yoder, John Howard, *The Original Revolution*. Scottdale, Pa.: Herald Press, 1972.

Yoder, John Howard. *The Politics of Jesus*. Grand Rapids, Mich.: Eerdmans, 1972.

Yoder, John Howard. *What Would You Do?: A Serious Answer to a Standard Question.* Scottdale, Pa.: Herald, 1983.

Yoder, John Howard. *When War Is Unjust: Being Honest in Just-War Thinking.* Minneapolis, Augsburg, 1984.

Zimmerman, Martha. *Should I Keep My Baby?* Minneapolis: Bethany, 1983.

Magazines, Journals, and Newsletters*

The Baptist Peacemaker, 1733 Bardstown Road, Louisville, KY 40205.

Bulletin of the Atomic Scientists, 5801 South Kenwood, Chicago, IL 60637.

The CALC Report. Published by Clergy and Laity Concerned.*

CCCO News Notes Covering War, Peace and Conscience. Published by The Central Committee for Conscientious Objectors, 2208 South Street, Philadelphia, PA 19146.

Center Peace. News Journal of the Center on Law and Pacifism, P.O. Box 1584, Colorado Springs, CO 80901.

Civilian-Based Defense: News and Opinion. Published by Association for Transarmament Studies, 3636 Lafayette Avenue, Omaha, NE 68131.

CNS Reports. Published by the Committee for National Security.

Conscience and Military Tax Campaign—U.S. Newsletter, 44 Bellhaven Road, Bellport, NY 11713.

The Defense Monitor. Published by the Center for Defense Information.

Disarmament Campaigns: An International Newsletter on Action Against the Arms Race. Postbus 18747, Anna Paulownaplein 3, 2502ES The Hague, Netherlands.

Disarming. Newsletter of the Riverside Church Disarmament Program, 490 Riverside Drive, New York, NY 10027.

Fellowship. Box 271, Nyack, NY 10960.

Friends Committee on National Legislation, Washington Newsletter. 245 Second Street, N.E., Washington, DC 20002.

Friends Journal. 1501 Cherry St. Dept. NT, Philadelphia, PA 19102.

---

*Addresses not included here are printed in the closing section of this appendix.

The Gandhi Message. Published by Mahatma Gandhi Memorial Foundation Inc., 4748 Western Avenue, P.O. Box 9515, Washington, DC 20016.

Global Perspectives. Newsletter of Center for Global Service and Education, Augsburg College, 731 21st Ave. S., Minneapolis, MN 55454.

Global Report. Newsletter of the Center for War/Peace Studies.

Human Life Issues. Published by the Human Life Center, St. John's University, Collegeville, MN 56321.

The Inter Dependent. Published by the United Nations Association, 300 East 42nd Street, New York, NY 10017.

The Mobilizer. Published by National Mobilization for Survival, 853 Broadway, New York, NY 10003.

Nuclear Times, Room 512, 298 Fifth Avenue, New York, NY 10001.

The Other Side, 300 West Apsley Street, Philadelphia, PA 19144.

P.S.—Prolifers for Survival Newsletter.

Peace Tax Fund Newsletter. Published by the National Campaign for a Peace Tax Fund, 2121 Decatur Place, N.W., Washington, DC 20008.

Peace Work: A New England Peace Movement Newsletter. Published by American Friends Service Committee.

PSR Newsletter. Published by Physicians for Social Responsibility.

RAR Newsletter. Published by the Interfaith Center to Reverse the Arms Race.

Sister Life. Newsletter published by Feminists for Life of America.

Sojourners, P.O. Box 29272, Washington, DC 20017.

Transnational Perspectives. Casa Postale 161, 1211 Geneve 16 Switzerland.

Update. Published by American Citizens Concerned for Life.

The Utney Reader: The Best of the Alternative Press, P.O. Box 19740, Marion, OH 43305.

World Federalist. Published by the World Federalist Association.

World Federalist News, Newsletter of the World Federalist Movement. Published by World Association of World Federalists.

World Policy Journal. Published by World Policy Institute.

World Press Review—News and Views from the Foreign Press, Box 915, Farmingdale, NY 11737.

Booklets and Pamphlets

Affirm Life: Pay for Peace. Handbook for World Peace Tax Fund Educators/Organizers. Available from Historic Peace Church Task Force on Taxes, Box 347, Newton, KS 67114.

Bedau, Hugo A. *The Case against the Death Penalty.* New York: ACLU, 1977. (ACLU, 22 East 40th St., New York, NY 10016.)

Berdyaev, Nicholas. *War and the Christian Conscience.* London: James Clarke & Co. Ltd., 1938.

Bernardin, Cardinal Joseph. *The Seamless Garment.* Available from National Catholic Reporter, P.O. Box 238, Kansas City, MO 64141

The Challenge of Peace; God's Promise and Our Response. The Catholic Bishops' Pastoral Letter. Available from U.S. Catholic Conference, 1312 Massachusetts Ave., N.W., Washington, DC 20005.

Chapter Handbook: How to Start a Lutherans for Life Chapter. Available from Lutherans for Life.

Cosby, Gordon and Price, Bill. *Handbook for World Peacemaker Groups,* and other *World Peace Papers.* Available from World Peacemakers.

Donaghy, John A. *Peacemaking and the Community of Faith: A Handbook for Congregations.* Published by the Fellowship of Reconciliation.

Durland, William. *People Pay for Peace: A Military Tax Refusal Guide for Radical Political Pacifists and People of Conscience.* Available from Center Peace Publishers, P.O. Box 1584, Colorado Springs, CO 80901.

Hudson, Richard. *The Case for the Binding Triad.* Available from Center for War/Peace Studies.

Irwin, Bob and Woodard, Beverly. *U.S. Defense Policy: Mainstream Views and Nonviolent Alternatives.* Available from International Seminars on Training for Nonviolent Action, Box 515, Waltham, MA 02254.

Johansen, Robert C. *Toward a Dependable Peace: A Proposal for an Appropriate Security System.* New York: Institute for World Order, 1978.

Johansen, Robert C. *Toward an Alternative Security System: Moving Beyond the Balance of Power in the Search for World Security.* New York: Institute for World Order, 1983.

Mandate for Peacemaking: A Statement of the American Lutheran Church. Available from the Office of Church and Society, the American Lutheran Church, 422 South 5th Street, Minneapolis, MN 55415.

Organizing against the Death Penalty: A Handbook, 2nd ed. National Coalition against the Death Penalty: 1501 Cherry St., Philadelphia, PA 19102.

Sharp, Gene. *Making the Abolition of War a Realistic Goal.* Available from the World Policy Institute.

Sivard, Ruth Leger. *World Military and Social Expenditures.* Published annually by World Priorities Inc., Box 1003, Leesburg, VA 22075.

Zehr, Howard. *Death as a Penalty.* Available from the Mennonite Central Committee, U.S. Office of Criminal Justice, 220 W. High St., Elkhart, IN 46516.

Audio-Video Resources

Audio Tapes

"A Case for Nonviolent Defense" by Gene Sharp. Catholic Education Center, Business Office, 328 West 6th Street, St. Paul, MN 55102.

"A Modern Alternative to War" and "More on Civilian-Based Defense" by Gene Sharp. "Common Ground," The Stanley Foundation, 420 East Third Street, Muscatine, IA 52761.

Video Tapes

"Alternatives to Violence," a five-part series featuring Gene Sharp and others. Available from WTL, Box 351(D), Primos, PA 19018.

"Blessed Are the Peacemakers," Part 1: A New Look at War, and Part 2: Christian Alternatives to War, by Lowell Erdahl. Available from Augsburg Publishing House, 426 South 5th St., Box 1209, Minneapolis, MN 55440.

"The Dream of an Impenetrable Shield; Ballistic Missile Defense in the Nuclear Age," by Barry M. Casper and Robert J. Goldman. This and other slide/audio materials available from Nuclear War Graphics Project, 100 Nevada Street, Northfield, MN 55057.

"Who Broke the Baby?" 30-minute video, especially for teenagers. Available from Lutherans for Life.

Organizations Providing Encouragement for Pro-life/Pro-peace Work

American Citizens Concerned for Life, 6127 Excelsior Boulevard, Minneapolis, MN 55416.

American Civil Liberties Union Capital Punishment Program, 132 West 43rd St., New York, NY 10036. Phone (212) 944-9800, Henry Schwarzchild.

American Friends Service Committee, 2161 Massachusetts Ave., Cambridge, MA 02140.

Amnesty International USA, 322 Eighth Ave., New York, NY 10001.

Birthright Inc., 63 South 9th St., Minneapolis, MN 55402.

Bread for the World, 802 Rhode Island Ave., N.E., Washington, DC 20018.

Capital Punishment Research Project, P.O. Drawer 277, 100 E. Main Street, Headland, AL 36346.

Center for Defense Information, 303 Capitol Gallery West, 600 Maryland Ave., S.W., Washington, DC 20024.

Center for War/Peace Studies, 218 E. 18th St., New York, NY 10003.

Clergy and Laity Concerned, 198 Broadway, New York, NY 10038.

Committee for National Security, 2000 P Street, N.W., Suite 515, Washington, DC 20036.

Council for a Liveable World, 11 Beacon Street, Boston, MA 02108.

Educators for Social Responsibility, 23 Garden Street, Cambridge, MA 02138.

Evangelicals for Social Action, P.O. Box 76560, Washington, DC 20013.

Fellowship of Reconciliation, Box 271, Nyack, NY 10960.

Feminists for Life of America, 811 East 47th Street, Kansas City, MO 64110.

Friends for a Non-violent World, 1925 Nicollet Avenue, Suite 101, Minneapolis, MN 55403.

Global Education Associates, 522 Park Ave., East Orange, NJ 07017.

Greenleaf Books, Weare, NH 03281. Source of Gandhi's writings and related works.

Ground Zero Minnesota, 101 University Ave. S.E., Minneapolis, MN 55414. Sponsors conferences and courses on human survival.

Institute for Defense and Disarmament Studies, 2001 Beacon Street, Brookline, MA 02146.

Institute for Policy Studies, 1901 Q Street, N.W., Washington, DC 20009. Publishes a periodic catalog of peace and justice literature.

Interfaith Center to Reduce the Arms Race, 132 North Euclid Ave., Pasadena, CA 91101.

The International Peace Institute, Radsugt, 4, Oslo 1, Norway.

International Physicians for the Prevention of Nuclear War, 225 Longwood Ave., Room 240, Boston, MA 02115. (Awarded the Nobel Peace Prize, 1985.)

Lutheran Peace Fellowship, 2481 Como Avenue., St. Paul, MN 55108.

Lutherans for Life, 275 North Syndicate, St. Paul, MN 55104.

The Martin Luther King Jr. Center for Nonviolent Social Change, 449 Auburn Ave., Atlanta, GA 30312.

The National Coalition Against the Death Penalty, 1501 Cherry St., Philadelphia, PA 19102.

National Peace Institute Foundation, 110 Maryland Ave., N.E, Washington, DC 20002.

National Right to Life Committee, 419-7th Street, N.W., Washington, DC 20004.

New Call to Peacemaking, A Cooperative Program of Brethren, Friends and Mennonites, Box 1245, Elkhart, IN 46515.

Pastoral Care Network for Social Responsibility, Hospital Box 1005 North Carolina Baptist Hospitals Inc., 300 S. Hawthorne Rd., Winston-Salem, NC 27103.

Pax Christi U.S.A., 348 East Tenth Street, Erie, PA 16503.

Physicians for Social Responsibility, 639 Massachusetts Ave., Cambridge, MA 02139.

Prolifers for Survival, P.O. Box 3316, Chapel Hill, NC 27515.

SANE: The Committee for a Sane Nuclear Policy, 711 G Street, S.E., Washington, DC 20003.

Stockholm International Peace Research Institute, Bergshamra, S-171 73 Solna, Sweden. Publishes yearbook on "World Armament and Disarmament."

Union of Concerned Scientists, 26 Church Street, Cambridge, MA 02238.

War Resisters League, 339 Lafayette Street, New York, NY 10012.

Wilmington College Peace Research Center, Pyle Center, Box 1183, Wilmington, OH 45177.

Women against Military Madness, 3255 Hennepin Ave., Minneapolis, MN 55408.

Women's Action for Nuclear Disarmament, Inc., P.O. Box 153, New Town Branch, Boston, MA 02258.

Women's International League for Peace and Freedom, 1213 Race Street, Philadelphia, PA 19107.

World Association of World Federalists, 410 South Michigan Avenue, Room 468, Chicago, IL 60605.

World Citizens, Inc., 5000 Girard Ave. S., Minneapolis, MN 55419.

World Federalist Association, 418 7th St. S.E., Washington, DC 20003.

World Peacemakers, 2025 Massachusetts Ave., N.W., Washington, DC 20036.

World Policy Institute, 777 United Nations Plaza, New York, NY 10017.

The World Watch Institute, 1776 Massachusetts Ave., N.W., Washington, DC 20036. Source of books and pamphlets by Lester Brown.

World without War Bookstore, 67 East Madison St., Chicago, IL 60603.

World without War Council, 421 South Wabash Avenue, Chicago, IL 60605. Source of "World without War Publications."